MongoDB for Java Developers

Design, build, and deliver efficient Java applications
using the most advanced NoSQL database

Francesco Marchioni

[PACKT]
PUBLISHING

BIRMINGHAM - MUMBAI

MongoDB for Java Developers

First published: August 2015

Production reference: 1070815

Published by Packt Publishing Ltd.
Livery Place
35 Livery Street
Birmingham B3 2PB, UK.

ISBN 978-1-78528-027-6

www.packtpub.com

Credits

Author
Francesco Marchioni

Reviewers
Daniel Mühlbachler

Weiwei Sun

Mehdi Tazi

Commissioning Editor
Veena Pagare

Acquisition Editors
James Jones

Nadeem N. Bagban

Content Development Editor
Neeshma Ramakrishnan

Technical Editor
Bharat Patil

Copy Editors
Merilyn Pereira

Laxmi Subramanian

Project Coordinator
Shweta Birwatkar

Proofreader
Safis Editing

Indexer
Tejal Soni

Production Coordinator
Aparna Bhagat

Cover Work
Aparna Bhagat

About the Author

Francesco Marchioni is a Red Hat Certified JBoss Administrator (RHCJA) and a Sun Certified enterprise architect working as a freelancer in Rome, Italy. He started learning Java in 1997, and since then, he has followed the path to the newest application program interfaces released by Sun. In 2000, he joined the JBoss community, when the application server was running the release 2.*X*.

He has spent many years as a software consultant, wherein he envisioned many successful software migrations from vendor platforms to open source products such as JBoss AS, fulfilling the tight budget requirements of current times.

Over the past 5 years, he has been authoring technical articles for OReilly Media and running an IT portal focused on JBoss products (`http://www.mastertheboss.com`).

In December 2009, he published *JBoss AS 5 Development*, which describes how to create and deploy Java Enterprise applications on JBoss AS (`http://www.packtpub.com/jboss-as-5-development/book`).

In December 2010, he published his second title, *JBoss AS 5 Performance Tuning*, which describes how to deliver fast and efficient applications on JBoss AS (`http://www.packtpub.com/jboss-5-performance-tuning/book`).

In December 2011, he published yet another title, *JBoss AS 7 Configuration, Deployment, and Administration*, which covers all the aspects of the newest application server release (`http://www.packtpub.com/jboss-as-7-configuration-deployment-administration/book`).

In June 2013, he authored a new title, *JBoss AS 7 Development*, which focuses on developing Java EE 6 API applications on JBoss AS 7 (`https://www.packtpub.com/application-development/jboss-7-development`).

About the Reviewers

Daniel Mühlbachler got interested in computer science shortly after entering high school, where he later developed web applications as part of a scholarship system for outstanding pupils.

He has profound knowledge of web development (PHP, HTML, CSS/LESS, and AngularJS), and has worked with a variety of other programming languages and systems, such as Java/Groovy, Grails, Objective-C and Swift, Matlab, C (with Cilk), Node.js, and Linux servers.

Furthermore, he works with some database management systems based on SQL and also some NoSQL systems, such as MongoDB and SOLR; this is also reflected in several projects that he is currently involved in at Catalysts GmbH.

After studying abroad as an exchange student in the United Kingdom, he completed his bachelor's degree at the Johannes Kepler University in Linz, Austria, with a thesis on aerosol satellite data processing for mobile visualization; this is where he also became familiar with processing large amounts of data.

Daniel enjoys solving challenging problems and is always keen on working with new technologies, especially related to the fields of big data, functional programming, optimization, and NoSQL databases.

More detailed information about his experience , as well as his contact details, can be found at www.muehlbachler.org and www.linkedin.com/in/danielmuehlbachler.

Weiwei Sun is a student of Southeast University, China, and also a student of Monash University, Australia. He also has a double master's degree in computer technology and information technology. He loves technology, programming, and open source projects.

HIs research interests are database technology, data visualization, and application of machine learning.

You can read more about him at `http://wwsun.github.com`.

Mehdi Tazi is a software engineer specializing in distributed information systems and agile project management.

His core expertise involves managing agile scrum teams, as well as architecting new solutions, and working with multiple technologies, such as JAVA/JEE, Spring, MongoDB, Cassandra, HTML5, Bootstrap, and AngularJS.

He has a degree in software engineering and a master's degree in business informatics. He also has several certifications, such as Core-Spring, MongoDB, Cassandra, and Scrum Master Official.

You can read more about him at `http://tazimehdi.com`.

www.PacktPub.com

Support files, eBooks, discount offers, and more

For support files and downloads related to your book, please visit www.PacktPub.com.

Did you know that Packt offers eBook versions of every book published, with PDF and ePub files available? You can upgrade to the eBook version at www.PacktPub.com and as a print book customer, you are entitled to a discount on the eBook copy. Get in touch with us at service@packtpub.com for more details.

At www.PacktPub.com, you can also read a collection of free technical articles, sign up for a range of free newsletters and receive exclusive discounts and offers on Packt books and eBooks.

https://www2.packtpub.com/books/subscription/packtlib

Do you need instant solutions to your IT questions? PacktLib is Packt's online digital book library. Here, you can search, access, and read Packt's entire library of books.

Why subscribe?
- Fully searchable across every book published by Packt
- Copy and paste, print, and bookmark content
- On demand and accessible via a web browser

Free access for Packt account holders

If you have an account with Packt at www.PacktPub.com, you can use this to access PacktLib today and view 9 entirely free books. Simply use your login credentials for immediate access.

*This book is dedicated to all the guys that patiently answered my questions
on MongoDB forums and to my son Alessandro that taught me
how to play 'Magic the Gathering' while waiting for replies*

Table of Contents

Preface

The NoSQL movement is growing in relevance, and it is attracting more and more developers. The MongoDB database is a well-recognized rising star in the NoSQL world. It is a document database that allows data to persist and query data in a nested state without any schema constraint and complex joins between documents. Understanding when it is appropriate to use MongoDB against a relational database and the interfaces to be used to interact with it requires some degree of experience.

This book provides all the knowledge to make MongoDB fit into your application schema, at the best of its capabilities. It starts from a basic introduction to the driver that can be used to perform some low level interaction with the storage. Then it moves on to use different patterns for abstracting the persistence layer into your applications, starting from the flexible Google JSON library, to the Hibernate OGM framework, and finally landing on the Spring Data framework.

What this book covers

Chapter 1, Introduction to MongoDB, covers the installation steps of MongoDB and its client tools and how to use the Mongo shell to perform basic database operations.

Chapter 2, Getting Started with Java Driver for MongoDB, introduces the Java Driver for MongoDB using a simple Java project developed with the NetBeans development environment.

Chapter 3, MongoDB CRUD Beyond the Basics, covers the advanced usage of the MongoDB Java driver such as data mapping, index creation, and bulk operations.

Chapter 4, MongoDB in the Java EE 7 Enterprise Environment, demonstrates how to create and deploy a Java Enterprise application that uses MongoDB as the storage.

Chapter 5, Managing Data Persistence with MongoDB and JPA, covers the development of a Java Enterprise application using Hibernate Object/Grid Mapper (OGM), which provides Java Persistence API (JPA) support for NoSQL databases.

Chapter 6, Building Applications for MongoDB with Spring Data, teaches you how to use Spring Data and Spring Boot to leverage micro services using MongoDB as the storage.

What you need for this book

The following software will be needed to run the examples contained in this book:

- Java Development Kit 1.7 or newer
- Mongo DB 2.6 or newer
- MongoDB JDBC Driver 2 and 3
- The NetBeans development environment (or equivalent)

All the software mentioned is freely available for downloading.

Who this book is for

This book is for Java developers and architects who want to learn how to develop Java applications using the most popular NoSQL solution and its use cases.

Conventions

In this book, you will find a number of styles of text that distinguish between different kinds of information. Here are some examples of these styles, and an explanation of their meaning.

Code words in text, database table names, folder names, filenames, file extensions, pathnames, dummy URLs, user input, and Twitter handles are shown as follows: "In command prompt, navigate to the `bin` directory present into the `mongodb` installation folder and point to the folder where data is stored."

A block of code is set as follows:

```
MongoClient mongoClient = new MongoClient( "localhost" , 27017 );
DB db = mongoClient.getDB( "test" );
System.out.println("Successfully connected to MongoDB");
```

When we wish to draw your attention to a particular part of a code block, the relevant lines or items are set in bold:

```
MongoClient mongoClient = new MongoClient( "localhost" , 27017 );
DB db = mongoClient.getDB( "test" );
System.out.println("Successfully connected to MongoDB");
```

Any command-line input or output is written as follows:

```
> db.users.find({}).sort({"name":1})

{ "_id" : ObjectId("5506d5708d7bd8471669e674"), "name" : "francesco",
"age" : 44, "phone" : "123-456-789" }
{ "_id" : ObjectId("550ad3ef89ef057ee0671652"), "name" : "owen", "age" :
32, "phone" : "555-444-333" }
```

New terms and **important words** are shown in bold. Words that you see on the screen, in menus or dialog boxes for example, appear in the text like this: " Now let's add a Java class to the project. From the **File** menu, select **Java Class** under **New** ".

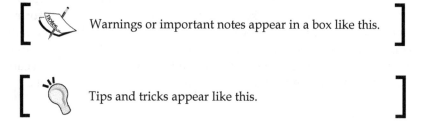

[Warnings or important notes appear in a box like this.]

[Tips and tricks appear like this.]

Reader feedback

Feedback from our readers is always welcome. Let us know what you think about this book—what you liked or may have disliked. Reader feedback is important for us to develop titles that you really get the most out of.

To send us general feedback, simply send an e-mail to feedback@packtpub.com, and mention the book title via the subject of your message.

If there is a topic that you have expertise in and you are interested in either writing or contributing to a book, see our author guide on www.packtpub.com/authors.

Customer support

Now that you are the proud owner of a Packt book, we have a number of things to help you to get the most from your purchase.

Downloading the example code

You can download the example code files for all Packt books you have purchased from your account at `http://www.packtpub.com`. If you purchased this book elsewhere, you can visit `http://www.packtpub.com/support` and register to have the files e-mailed directly to you.

Errata

Although we have taken every care to ensure the accuracy of our content, mistakes do happen. If you find a mistake in one of our books—maybe a mistake in the text or the code—we would be grateful if you would report this to us. By doing so, you can save other readers from frustration and help us improve subsequent versions of this book. If you find any errata, please report them by visiting `http://www.packtpub.com/submit-errata`, selecting your book, clicking on the **errata submission form** link, and entering the details of your errata. Once your errata are verified, your submission will be accepted and the errata will be uploaded on our website, or added to any list of existing errata, under the Errata section of that title. Any existing errata can be viewed by selecting your title from `http://www.packtpub.com/support`.

Piracy

Piracy of copyright material on the Internet is an ongoing problem across all media. At Packt, we take the protection of our copyright and licenses very seriously. If you come across any illegal copies of our works, in any form, on the Internet, please provide us with the location address or website name immediately so that we can pursue a remedy.

Please contact us at `copyright@packtpub.com` with a link to the suspected pirated material.

We appreciate your help in protecting our authors, and our ability to bring you valuable content.

Questions

You can contact us at `questions@packtpub.com` if you are having a problem with any aspect of the book, and we will do our best to address it.

1
Introduction to MongoDB

In this book, you will learn how to develop Java applications using the MongoDB database, which is an open source document-oriented database, recognized as a rising star in the NoSQL world. In a nutshell, MongoDB is a document database, which allows data to persist in a nested state, and importantly, it can query that nested data in an ad hoc fashion. It enforces no schema, so documents can optionally contain fields or types that no other document in the collection contains.

The focus of this book is on applications development; however, we will at first gather all the resources to connect to MongoDB and add a quick introduction to the world of NoSQL databases. We will cover the following topics in more detail:

- A bird's eye view of the NoSQL landscape
- Installing MongoDB and client tools
- Using the MongoDB shell

Getting into the NoSQL movement

NoSQL is a generic term used to refer to any data store that does not follow the traditional RDBMS model—specifically, the data is nonrelational and it generally does not use SQL as a query language. Most of the databases that are categorized as NoSQL focus on availability and scalability in spite of atomicity or consistency.

This seems quite a generic definition of NoSQL databases; however, all databases that fall into this category have some characteristics in common such as:

- **Storing data in many formats**: Almost all RDBMS databases are based on the storage or rows in tables. NoSQL databases, on the other hand, can use different formats such as document stores, graph databases, key-value stores and even more.

- **Joinless**: NoSQL databases are able to extract your data using simple document-oriented interfaces without using SQL joins.

- **Schemaless data representation**: A characteristic of NoSQL implementations is that they are based on a schemaless data representation, with the notable exception of the Cassandra database (`http://cassandra.apache.org/`). The advantage of this approach is that you don't need to define a data structure beforehand, which can thus continue to change over time.

- **Ability to work with many machines**: Most NoSQL systems buy you the ability to store your database on multiple machines while maintaining high-speed performance. This brings the advantage of leveraging low cost machines with separate RAM and disk and also supports linear scalability.

On the other hand, all database developers and administrators know the ACID acronym. It says that database transactions should be:

- **Atomicity**: Everything in a transaction either succeeds or is rolled back

- **Consistency**: Every transaction must leave the database in a consistent state

- **Isolation**: Each transaction that is running cannot interfere with other transactions

- **Durability**: A completed transaction gets persisted, even after applications restart

At first glance, these qualities seem vital. In practice, however, for many applications, they are incompatible with the availability and performance in very large environments. As an example, let's suppose that you have developed an online book store and you want to display how many of each book you have in your inventory. Each time a user is in the process of buying a book, you need to lock part of the database until they finish so that every visitors from the world will see the exact inventory numbers. That works just fine for a small homemade site but not if you run Amazon.com. For this reason, when we talk about NoSQL databases, or, generally, if we are designing distributed systems, we might have to look beyond the traditional ACID properties. As stated by the CAP theorem, coined by Eric Brewer, the following set of requirements are truly essential when designing applications for distributed architectures:

- **Consistency**: This means the database mostly remains adherent to its rules (constraints, triggers, and so on) after the execution of each operation and that any future transaction will see the effects of the earlier transactions committed. For example, after executing an update, all the clients see the same data.

- **Availability**: Each operation is guaranteed a response — a successful or failed execution. This, in practice, means no downtime.

- **Partition tolerance**: This means the system continues to function even if the communication among the servers is temporarily unreliable (for example, the servers involved in the transaction may be partitioned into multiple groups, which cannot communicate with one another).

In practice, as it is theoretically impossible to have all three requirements met, a combination of two must be chosen and this is usually the deciding factor in what technology is used, as shown in the following figure:

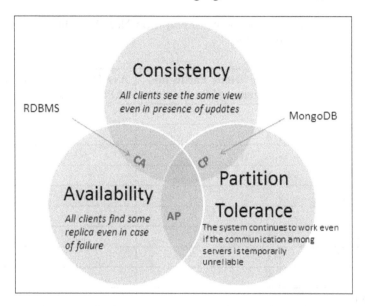

If you are designing a typical web application that uses a SQL database, most likely, you are in the **CA** part of the diagram. This is because a traditional RDBMS is typically transaction-based (**C**) and it can be highly available (**A**). However, it cannot be **Partition Tolerance** (**P**) because SQL databases tend to run on single nodes.

MongoDB, on the other hand, is consistent by default (C). This means if you perform a write on the database followed by a read, you will be able to read the same data (assuming that the write was successful).

Besides consistency, MongoDB leverages Partition Tolerance (P) by means of replica sets. In a replica set, there exists a single primary node that accepts writes, and asynchronously replicates a log of its operations to other secondary databases.

However, not all NoSQL databases are built with the same focus. An example of this is CouchDB. Just like MongoDB, it is document oriented and has been built to scale across multiple nodes easily; on the other hand, while MongoDB (CP) favors consistency, CouchDB favors availability (AP) in spite of consistency. CouchDB uses a replication model called **Eventual Consistency**. In this model, clients can write data to one database node without waiting for acknowledgment from other nodes. The system takes care to copy document changes between nodes, so that they can eventually be in sync.

The following table summarizes the most common NoSQL databases and their position relative to CAP attributes:

Database	Consistent, Partition-Tolerant (CP)	Available, Partition-Tolerant (AP)
BigTable	X	
Hypertable	X	
HBase	X	
MongoDB	X	
Terrastore	X	
Redis	X	
Scalaris	X	
MemcacheDB	X	
Berkeley DB	X	
Dynamo		X
Voldemort		X
Tokyo Cabinet		X
KAI		X
Cassandra		X
CouchDB		X
SimpleDB		X
Riak		X

Comparing RDBMS and NoSQL databases

As you might guess, there is no absolute winner between traditional databases and the new NoSQL standard. However, we can identify a set of pros and cons related to each technology. This can lead to a better understanding of which one is most fit for our scenarios. Let's start from traditional RDBMS:

RDBMS pros	RDBMS cons
ACID transactions at the database level make development easier.	The object-relational mapping layer can be complex.
Fine-grained security on columns and rows using views prevents views and changes by unauthorized users. Most SQL code is portable to other SQL databases, including open source options.	RDBMS doesn't scale out when joins are required.
Typed columns and constraints will validate data before it's added to the database and increase data quality.	Sharding over many servers can be done but requires application code and will be operationally inefficient.
The existing staff members are already familiar with entity-relational design and SQL.	Full-text search requires third-party tools.
Well-consolidated theoretical basis and design rules.	Storing high-variability data in tables can be challenging.

The following is a table that contains the advantages and disadvantages of NoSQL databases:

NoSQL pros	NoSQL cons
It can store complex data types (such as documents) in a single item of storage.	There is a lack of server-side transactions; therefore, it is not fit for inherently transactional systems.
It allows horizontal scalability, which does not require you to set up complex joins and data can be easily partitioned and processed in parallel.	Document stores do not provide fine-grained security at the element level.
It saves on development time as it is not required to design a fine-grained data model.	NoSQL systems are new to many staff members and additional training may be required.
It is quite fast for inserting new data and for simple operations or queries.	The document store has its own proprietary nonstandard query language, which prohibits portability.
It provides support for Map/Reduce, which is a simple paradigm that allows for scaling computation on a cluster of computing nodes.	There is an absence of standardization. No standard APIs or query languages. It means that migration to a solution from different vendors is more costly. Also, there are no standard tools (for example, for reporting).

Living without transactions

As you can imagine, one of the most important factors when deciding to use MongoDB or traditional RDBMS is the need for transactions.

With an RDBMS, you can update the database in sophisticated ways using SQL and wrap multiple statements in a transaction to get atomicity and rollback. MongoDB doesn't support transactions. This is a solid tradeoff based on MongoDB's goal of being simple, fast, and scalable. MongoDB, however, supports a range of atomic update operations that can work on the internal structures of a complex document. So, for example, by including multiple structures within one document (such as arrays), you can achieve an update in a single atomic way, just like you would do with an ordinary transaction.

 As documents can grow in complexity and contain several nested documents, single-document atomicity can be used as a replacement for transactions in many scenarios.

On the other hand, operations that includes multiple documents (often referred to as multi-document transactions), are conversely not atomic.

In such scenarios, when you need to synchronize multi-document transactions, you can implement the 2PC (two-phase commit) in your application so that you can provision these kinds of multidocument updates. Discussing about this pattern, however, is out of the scope of this book, but if you are eager to know more, you can learn more from `http://docs.mongodb.org/manual/tutorial/perform-two-phase-commits/`.

So, to sum it up, if your application's requirements can be met via document updates (also by using nested documents to provide an atomic update), then this is a perfect use case for MongoDB, which will allow a much easier horizontal scaling of your application.

On the other hand, if strict transaction semantics (such as a banking application) are required, then nothing can beat a relational database. In some scenarios, you can combine both approaches (RDBMS and MongoDB) to get the best of both worlds, at the price of a more complex infrastructure to maintain. Such hybrid solutions are quite common; however, you can see them in production apps such as the New York Times website.

Managing read-write concurrency

In RDBMS, managing the execution of concurrent work units is a fundamental concept. The underlying implementation of each database uses behind the scenes locks or Multiversion control to provide the isolation of each work unit. On the other hand, MongoDB uses reader/writer locks that allow concurrent readers shared access to a resource, such as a database or collection, but give exclusive access to a single write operation. In more detail here is how MongoDB handles read and write locks:

- There can be an unlimited number of simultaneous readers on a database

- There can only be one writer at a time on any collection in any one database

- The writers block out the readers once a write request comes in; all the readers are blocked until the write completes (which is also known as writer-greedy)

Since version 2.2 of MongoDB, it is possible to restrict the scope of the lock just the database the read or write operation was working with. If you are using MongoDB 3.0 or later, the scope of the lock is pulled in further than ever before. Now, when a write is occurring, only the documents involved in the write operation will be locked. In order to store information about locks, MongoDB relies on a storage engine, which is a part of the database and is responsible for managing how data is stored on the disk. In particular, MongoDB 3.0 comes with two storage engines:

- **MMAPv1**: This is the default storage engine, which uses collection-level locking

- **WiredTiger**: This is the new storage engine, which ships with document-level locking and compression (only available for the 64-bit version)

 By using the WiredTiger storage engine, all write operations happen within the context of a document-level lock. As a result, multiple clients can modify more than one document in a single collection at the same time. Thanks to this granular concurrency control, MongoDB can more effectively support workloads with read, write, and updates, as well as high-throughput concurrent workloads.

MongoDB core elements

In order to understand the capabilities of MongoDB, you need to learn the core elements the database is composed of. Actually, MongoDB is organized with a set of building blocks, which include the following:

- **Database**: This is, just like for the database, the top-level element. However, a relational database contains (mostly) tables and views. A Mongo Database, on the other hand, is a physical container of a structure called a collection. Each database has its own set of files on the filesystem. A single MongoDB server typically has multiple databases.

- **Collection**: This is a set of MongoDB documents. A collection is the equivalent of an RDBMS table. There can be only one collection with that name on the database but obviously multiple collections can coexist in a database. Typically, the collections contained in a database are related, although they do not enforce a schema as RDBMS tables do.

- **Documents**: This is the most basic unit of data in MongoDB. Basically, it is composed by a set of key-value pairs. Unlike database records, documents have a dynamic schema, which means documents that are part of the same collection do not need to have the same set of fields. Much the same way, the fields contained in a document may hold different data types.

The following diagram summarizes the concepts we just discussed:

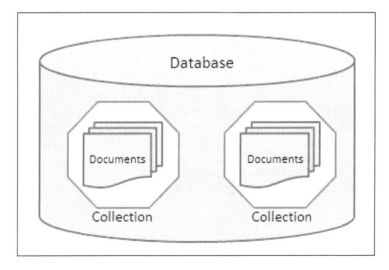

The heart of MongoDB – the document

At the heart of MongoDB is the document, an ordered set of keys with associated values. The representation of a document varies by the programming language, but most languages have a data structure that is a natural fit, such as a map, hash, or dictionary. Here is a very basic example of a document, which is understood by MongoDB:

```
{"name" : "Francesco",
 "age" : 44,
 "phone":"123-567-890"}
```

Most documents will be more complex than this simple one and will often contain embedded data within them. These denormalized data models allow applications to retrieve and manipulate related data in a single database operation:

```
{"name" : "Francesco",
 "age" : 44,
 "contact" : {
    "phone":"123-567-890"
  }
}
```

As you can see from the preceding example, we have included the contact information within the same document by using an embedded document with a single key named contact.

Each document requires a key, which needs to be unique within a document. The keys contained in a document are strings. Any UTF-8 character can be included in a key, with a few exceptions:

- You cannot include the character \0 (also known as the null character) in a key. This character is used to indicate the end of a key.
- The . and $ characters are internally used by the database so they should be used only in limited cases. As a general rule, it is better to completely avoid using these characters as most MongoDB drivers can generate exceptions when they are used inappropriately.

Finally, you need to be aware that MongoDB is both type-sensitive and case-sensitive. For example, these documents are distinct:

```
{"age" : 18}
{"age" : "18"}
```

The same applies to the following documents:

```
{"age" : 18}
{"Age" : 18}
```

Understanding how MongoDB stores data

The sample documents you have seen so far should be familiar to you if you have ever heard about **JavaScript Object Notation (JSON)**. JSON is a human and machine-readable open standard that simplifies data interchange and is also one of the most used formats for data interchange in applications along with XML. JSON is able to deal with all the basic data types used by applications such as String, numbers, Boolean values, as well as arrays and hashes. MongoDB is able to store JSON documents into its collections to store records. Let's see an example of a JSON document:

```
{
  _id":1,
  "name":{
    "first":"Dennis",
    "last":"Ritchie"
  },
  "contribs":[
    "Altran",
    "B",
    "C",
    "Unix"
  ],
  "awards":[
    {
      "award":"Turing Award",
      "year":1983
    },
    {
      "award":"National medal of technology",
      "year":1999
    }
  ]
}
```

A JSON-based database returns a set of data that can be easily parsed by most programming languages such as Java, Python, JavaScript, and others, reducing the amount of code you need to build into your application layer.

Behind the scenes, MongoDB represents JSON documents using a binary-encoded format called **BSON**. Documents encoded with BSON enhance the JSON data model to provide additional data types and efficiency when encoding/decoding data within different languages.

MongoDB uses a fast and lightweight BSON implementation, which is highly traversable and supports complex structures such as embedded objects and arrays.

Data types accepted in documents

So far, we have used just two basic data types, String and Integer. MongoDB offers a wide choice of data types, which can be used in your documents:

- **String**: This is the most common data type as it contains a string of text (such as: `"name": "John"`).

- **Integer (32 bit and 64-bit)**: This type is used to store a numerical value (for example, `"age" : 40`). Note that an Integer requires no quotes to be placed before or after the Integer.

- **Boolean**: This data type can be used to store either a TRUE or a FALSE value.

- **Double**: This data type is used to store floating-point values.

- **Min/Max keys**: This data type is used to compare a value against the lowest and highest BSON elements, respectively.

- **Arrays**: This type is used to store arrays or list or multiple values into one key (for example, `["John, Smith","Mark, Spencer"]`).

- **Timestamp**: This data type is used to store a timestamp. This can be useful to store when a document has been last modified or created.

- **Object**: This data type is used for storing embedded documents.

- **Null**: This data type is used for a null value.

- **Symbol**: This data type allows storing characters such as String; however, it's generally used by languages that use a specific symbol type.

- **Date**: This data type allows storing the current date or time in the Unix time format (POSIX time).

- **Object ID**: This data type is used to store the document's ID.

- **Binary data**: This data type is used to store a binary set of data.

- **Regular expression**: This data type is used for regular expressions. All options are represented by specific characters provided in alphabetical order. You will learn more about regular expressions.

- **JavaScript code**: This data type is used for JavaScript code.

Installing and starting MongoDB

Installing Mongo DB is much easier than most RDBMS as it's just a matter of unzipping the archived database and, if necessary, configure a new path for data storage. Let's look at the installation for different operating system architectures.

Installing MongoDB on Windows

For installing MongoDB on Windows, perform the following steps:

1. Download the latest stable release of MongoDB from `http://www.mongodb.org/downloads`. (At the time of writing, the latest stable release is 3.0.3, which is available as Microsoft Installer or as a ZIP file). Ensure you download the correct version of MongoDB for your Windows system.

2. Execute the MSI Installer, or if you have downloaded MongoDB as a ZIP file, simply extract the downloaded file to `C:\drive` or any other location.

MongoDB requires a data directory to store its files. The default location for the MongoDB data folder on Windows is `c:\data\db`. Execute the following command from the command prompt to create the default folder:

```
C:\mongodb-win32-x86_64-3.0.3>md data
```

In Command Prompt, navigate to the `bin` directory present in the `mongodb` installation folder and point to the folder where data is stored:

```
C:\mongodb-win32-x86_64-3.0.3\bin> mongod.exe   --dbpath "C:\mongodb-win32-x86_64-3.0.3\data"
```

This will show the `waiting for the connections` message on the console output, which indicates that the `mongod.exe` process is running successfully.

Installing MongoDB on Linux

The installation on Linux can be different depending on your Linux distribution. Here is a general-purpose installation process:

1. Download the latest MongoDB distribution, which is appropriate for your OS architecture:

   ```
   curl -O https://fastdl.mongodb.org/linux/mongodb-linux-x86_64-
   3.0.3.tgz
   ```

2. Extract the downloaded files:

   ```
   tar -zxvf mongodb-linux-x86_64-3.0.3.tgz
   ```

3. Copy files to a target directory:

   ```
   mkdir -p mongodb
   cp -R -n mongodb-linux-x86_64-3.0.3/ mongodb
   ```

4. Include MongoDB scripts in the system's PATH variable:

   ```
   export PATH=<mongodb-install-directory>/bin:$PATH
   ```

5. Just like we did for Windows, we will create the data folder:

   ```
   mkdir -p /data/db
   ```

6. Now, you can start MongoDB much the same way as with Windows:

   ```
   mongod --dbpath /data/db
   ```

MongoDB start up options

The list of start up options, which can be applied to the mongod server is quite large and is detailed at http://docs.mongodb.org/manual/reference/program/mongod/.

The following table summarizes the most common options for a handy reference:

Option	Description
--help, -h	This returns the information on the options and use of mongod.
--version	This returns the mongod release number.
--config <filename>	This specifies the configuration file to be used by mongod.
--port <port>	This specifies the TCP listening port on which MongoDB listens. (the default is 27017)
--bind_ip <ip address>	This specifies the IP address that mongod binds to in order to listen for connections from applications (the default is All interfaces.).
--logpath <path>	This sends all diagnostic logging information to a log file instead of to a standard output or to the host's syslog system.
--logappend	This appends new entries to the end of the log file rather than overwriting the content of the log when the mongod instance restarts.
--httpinterface	This enables the HTTP interface. Enabling the interface can increase network exposure.
--fork	This enables a daemon mode that runs the mongod process in the background. By default, mongod does not run as a daemon.
--auth	This enables authorization to control the user's access to database resources and operations. When authorization is enabled, MongoDB requires all clients to authenticate themselves first in order to determine the access for the client.
--noauth	This disables authentication. It is currently the default and exists for future compatibility and clarity.
--rest	This enables the simple REST API. Enabling the REST API enables the HTTP interface, even if the HTTP interface option is disabled, and as a result can increase network exposure.

Option	Description
`--profile <level>`	This changes the level of database profiling (0 Off, which means no profiling; 1 On, which only includes slow operations; and 2 On, which includes all the operations.)
`--shutdown`	This safely terminates the mongod process. It is available only on Linux systems.

In addition, the following options can be used to vary the storage of the database:

Option	Description
`--dbpath <path>`	This is the directory where the mongod instance stores its data. The default is `/data/db` on Linux and OS X and `C:\data\db` on Windows.
`--storageEngine string`	This specifies the storage engine for the mongod database. The valid options include `mmapv1` and `wiredTiger`. The default is `mmapv1`.
`--directoryperdb`	This stores each database's files in its own folder in the `data` directory. When applied to an existing system, the `--directoryperdb` option alters the storage pattern of the data directory.

Troubleshooting MongoDB installation

On startup, the server will print some version and system information and then begin waiting for connections. By default, MongoDB listens for connections on port 27017. The server process will fail to start if the port is already used by another process — the most common cause of it is that another instance of MongoDB is already running on your machine.

> You can stop mongod by typing *Ctrl* + *C* in the shell that is running the server. In a clean shutdown, the mongod process completes all running operations, flushes all data to files, and closes all data files. Within the *Securing database access* section of this chapter, we show how to use the Mongo shell to shut down the database from the Mongo shell.

The `mongod` command also launches a basic HTTP server that listens, by default, on port 28017. This web server can be used to capture REST request (see `http://docs.mongodb.org/ecosystem/tools/http-interfaces/`) and to query for administrative information about your database by pointing to `http://localhost:28017` with your web browser.

 You need to start mongod with the `--rest` option in order to enable the web administration console.

The following screenshot depicts the web administration GUI when executed from the browser:

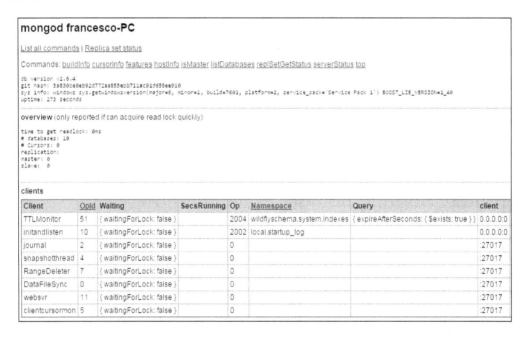

Mongo tools

MongoDB ships with a set of shell commands, which can be useful to administrate your server. We will shortly provide a description of each command, so that you can get an initial introduction to the server administration:

- `bsondump`: This displays BSON files in a human-readable format
- `mongoimport`: This converts data from JSON, TSV, or CSV and stores them into a collection

- `mongoexport`: This writes an existing collection using the CSV or JSON formats
- `mongodump`/`mongorestore`: This dumps MongoDB data to disk using the BSON format (`mongodump`), or restores them (`mongorestore`) to a live database
- `mongostat`: This monitors running MongoDB servers, replica sets, or clusters
- `mongofiles`: This reads, writes, deletes, or updates files in GridFS
- `mongooplog`: This replays oplog entries between MongoDB servers
- `mongotop`: This monitors data reading/writing on a running Mongo server

Here is an example of how to use the `mongoimport` tool to import a CSV-formatted data contained in `/var/data/users.csv` into the collection `users` in the sample database on the MongoDB instance running on the localhost port numbered 27017:

```
mongoimport --db sample --collection users --type csv --headerline --file
/var/data/users.csv
```

In the preceding example, `mongoimport` determines the name of files using the first line in the CSV file, because of `--headerline`.

If you want to export the MongoDB documents, you can use the `mongoexport` tool. Let's look at an example of how to export the collection `users` (part of the sampled database), limited to the first 100 records:

```
mongoexport --db sampledb --collection users --limit 100 --out export.
json
```

As part of your daily backup strategy, you should consider using the `mongodump` tool, which is a utility for creating a binary export of the contents of a database.

 `mongodump` does not provide a backup of the local database.

The following command creates a database dump for the collection named `users` contained in the database named `sampled`. In this case, the database is running on the local interface on port 27017:

```
mongodump  --db test --collection users
```

The preceding command will create a BSON binary file named `users.bson` and a JSON file named `users.metadata.json` containing the documents. The files will be created under `dump/[database-name]`.

Finally, the `mongorestore` program loads binary data from a database dump created by `mongodump` to a MongoDB instance. `mongorestore` can both create a new database and add data to an existing database:

```
mongorestore --collection users --db sampledb dump/sampledb/users.bson
```

Introduction to the MongoDB shell

MongoDB ships with a JavaScript shell that allows interaction with a MongoDB instance from the command line. The shell is the bread-and-butter tool for performing administrative functions, monitoring a running instance, or just inserting documents.

To start the shell, run the `mongo` executable:

```
$ mongo
MongoDB shell version: 3.0.3
connecting to: test
```

The shell automatically attempts to connect to a running MongoDB server on startup, so make sure you start mongod before starting the shell.

If no other database is specified on startup, the shell selects a default database called `test`. As a way of keeping all the subsequent tutorial exercises under the same namespace, let's start by switching to the `sampledb` database:

```
> use sampledb
switched to db sampledb
```

If you are coming from an RDBMS background, you might be surprised that we can switch to a new database without formerly creating it. The point is that creating the database is not required in MongoDB. Databases and collections are first created when documents are actually inserted. Hence, individual collections and databases can be created at runtime just as the structure of a document is known.

If you want to check the list of available databases, then you can use the `show dbs` command:

```
>show dbs
local      0.78125GB
test       0.23012GB
```

As you can see, the database we created (`sampledb`) is not present in the list. To display the database, you need to insert at least one document into it. The next section will show you how to do it.

Inserting documents

As we said, MongoDB documents can be specified in the JSON format. For example, let's recall the simple document that we have already introduced:

```
{"name" : "francesco",
 "age" : 44,
 "phone":"123-567-890"
}
```

In order to insert this document, you need to choose a collection where the document will be stored. Here's how you can do it with the Mongo shell:

```
db.users.insert({"name": "francesco","age": 44, "phone": "123-567-890"})
```

As for databases, collections can be created dynamically by specifying it into the insert statement. Congratulations, you've just saved your first document!

 MongoDB supports a special kind of collection named Capped collections, which are fixed-size collections that are able to support high-throughput operations where insert and retrieve documents are based on insertion order. Capped collections need to be created first before being able to use them. We will show you how to use Capped collections in the next chapter, using the Java driver.

Querying documents

The find method is used to perform queries in MongoDB. If no argument is given to the find method, it will return all the documents contained in the collection as in the following statement:

```
> db.users.find()
```

The response will look something like this:

```
{ "_id" : ObjectId("5506d5988d7bd8471669e675"), "name" : "francesco", "age" : 44, "phone" : "123-456-789" }
```

Maybe you have noticed that the _id field has been added to the document. This is a special key that works like a primary key. As a matter of fact, every MongoDB document requires a unique identifier and if you don't provide one in your document, then a special MongoDB ID will be generated and added to the document at that time.

Now, let's include another user in our collections so that we can refine our searches:

```
> db.users.insert({"name": "owen","age": 32, "phone": "555-444-333"})
```

Your collection should now include two documents, as verified by the count function:

```
> db.users.count()
2
```

 As you can see from the preceding insert command, document keys are specified with quotes. This is not mandatory but generally a good practice as it makes queries more readable.

Having two documents in our collection, we will learn how to add a query selector to our find statement so that we filter users based on a key value. For example, here is how to find a user whose name is owen:

```
> db.users.find({"name": "owen"})
{ "_id" : ObjectId("5506eea18d7bd8471669e676"), "name" : "owen",
"age" : 32, "phone" : "555-444-333" }
```

Multiple conditions can be specified within a query, just like you would do with a WHERE – AND construct in SQL:

```
> db.users.find({"name": "owen", "age": 32})

{ "_id" : ObjectId("5506eea18d7bd8471669e676"), "name" : "owen",
"age" : 32, "phone" : "555-444-333" }
```

Choosing the keys to return

The queries mentioned earlier are equivalent to a SELECT * statement in SQL terms. You can use a projection to select a subset of fields to return from each document in a query result set. This can be especially useful when you are selecting large documents, as it will reduce the costs of network latency and deserialization.

Projections are commonly activated by means of binary operators (0,1); the binary operator *0* means that the key must not be included in the search whilst *1* obviously means that the key has to be included. Here is an example of how to include the name and age keys in the fields to be returned (along with the id field, which is always included by default:

```
> db.users.find({}, {"name": 1,"age": 1})
```

```
{ "_id" : ObjectId("5506d5988d7bd8471669e675"), "name" : "francesco",
"age" : 44  }
{ "_id" : ObjectId("5506eea18d7bd8471669e676"), "name" : "owen", "age" :
32 }
```

By setting the projection values for the name and age to 0, the phone number is returned instead:

```
> db.users.find({}, {"name": 0,"age": 0})
{ "_id" : ObjectId("5506d5988d7bd8471669e675"), "phone" : "123-456-789" }
{ "_id" : ObjectId("5506eea18d7bd8471669e676"), "phone" : "555-444-333" }
```

 Note that you cannot have a mix of inclusions and exclusions in your projection. The exception to the rule is the _id field. In fact, {_id: 0, name: 1, age: 1} works but any inclusion/exclusion combination of other fields does not.

Using ranges in your queries

Quite commonly, your queries will use some functions to restrict the range of the returned data, which is done in most SQL dialects and languages with the > and < or = operators.

The equivalent operators in MongoDB terms are $gt, $gte, $lt, and $lte. Here is how to find users whose age is greater than *40* using the $gt operator:

```
> db.users.find({ age: { $gt: 40 } })


{ "_id" : ObjectId("5506d5988d7bd8471669e675"), "name" : "francesco",
"age" : 44, "phone" : "123-456-789" }
```

The $gte operator, on the other hand, is able to select keys that are greater than or equal (>=) to the one specified:

```
> db.users.find({ age: { $gte: 32 } })


{ "_id" : ObjectId("5506d5988d7bd8471669e675"), "name" : "francesco",
"age" : 44, "phone" : "123-456-789" }
{ "_id" : ObjectId("5506eea18d7bd8471669e676"), "name" : "owen",
"age" : 32, "phone" : "555-444-333" }
```

The $lt and $lte operators, on the other hand, allow you to select keys which are smaller and smaller/equal to the value specified.

Using logical operators to query data

You cannot think of a scripting language without logical operators and MongoDB is no exception. The most common logical operators are named $or, $and, and $not in MongoDB.

We will not enter into the basics of logical operators, rather let's see a concrete example of the logical operator OR:

```
db.users.find( { $or: [ { "age": { $lt: 35 } }, { "name": "john" } ]
} )
```

In the preceding query, we are selecting users whose age is smaller than 35 or have the name john. As one of the conditions evaluates to true, it will return one user:

```
{ "_id" : ObjectId("5506eea18d7bd8471669e676"), "name" : "owen",
"age" : 32, "phone" : "555-444-333" }
```

By turning to the AND logical operator, on the other hand, no users will be returned:

```
db.users.find( { $and: [ { "age": { $lt: 35 } }, { "name": "john" } ] } )
```

By using the NOT operator, you can invert the effect of a query expression and return documents that do not match the query expression. For example, if you wanted to query for all users with last names not beginning with f, you could use $not as follows:

```
> db.users.find({"name": {$not: /^f/} })
{ "_id" : ObjectId("5506eea18d7bd8471669e676"), "name" : "owen", "age" :
32, "phone" : "555-444-333" }
```

> **Using LIKE in Mongo**
>
>
>
> Note the /expr/ operator, which can be used to achieve a SQL-like equivalent expression. For example, in its simplest form, you can use it to query for phone numbers, which are like 444:
>
> ```
> > db.users.find({"phone": /444/})
> ```

Updating documents

In order to update an existing document, you need to provide two arguments:

- The document to update
- How the selected documents should be modified

Let's see a practical example, supposing that you wanted to change the key age for the user owen to be 39:

```
> db.users.update({name: "owen"}, {$set: {"age": 39}})


WriteResult({ "nMatched" : 1, "nUpserted" : 0, "nModified" : 1 })
```

The outcome of the statement informs us that the update matched one document which was modified. A find issued on the users collection reveals that the change has been applied:

```
> db.users.find()


{ "_id" : ObjectId("5506d5988d7bd8471669e675"), "name" : "francesco",
"age" : 44, "phone" : "123-456-789" }
{ "_id" : ObjectId("5506eea18d7bd8471669e676"), "name" : "owen", "age" :
39, "phone" : "555-444-333" }
```

> Be aware that executing an update without the $set operator won't update the fields but replace the whole document, while preserving the _id field.

The update supports an additional option, which can be used to perform a more complex logic. For example, what if you wanted to update the record if it exists, and create it if it doesn't? This is called upsert and can be achieved by setting the upsert option to true, as in the following command line:

```
> db.users.update({user: "frank"}, {age: 40},{ upsert: true} )


WriteResult({
        "nMatched" : 0,
        "nUpserted" : 1,
        "nModified" : 0,
        "_id" : ObjectId("55082f5ea30be312eb167fcb")
})
```

As you can see from the output, an upsert has been executed and a document with the age key has been added:

```
> db.users.find()


{ "_id" : ObjectId("5506d5988d7bd8471669e675"), "name" : "francesco",
"age" : 44, "phone" : "123-456-789" }
```

```
{ "_id" : ObjectId("5506eea18d7bd8471669e676"), "name" : "owen", "age" :
39, "phone" : "555-444-333" }
{ "_id" : ObjectId("55082f5ea30be312eb167fcb"), "age" : 40 }
```

Updating a document with MongoDB can be done also on a portion of a document, for example, you can remove a single key from your collection by using the $unset option. In the following update, we are removing the age key to all documents whose name key equals to owen.

```
> db.users.update({name: "owen"}, {$unset : { "age" : 1} })
```

```
WriteResult({ "nMatched" : 1, "nUpserted" : 0, "nModified" : 1 })
```

Executing the find on our collection confirms the update:

```
> db.users.find()
```

```
{ "_id" : ObjectId("5506d5988d7bd8471669e675"), "name" : "francesco",
"age" : 44, "phone" : "123-456-789" }
{ "_id" : ObjectId("5506eea18d7bd8471669e676"), "name" : "owen", "phone"
: "555-444-333" }
{ "_id" : ObjectId("55082f5ea30be312eb167fcb"), "age" : 40 }
```

The opposite of the $unset operator is $push, which allows you to append a value to a specified field. So here is how you can restore the age key for the user owen:

```
> db.users.update({name: "owen"}, {$push : { "age" : 39} })
WriteResult({ "nMatched" : 1, "nUpserted" : 0, "nModified" : 1 })
```

 You can achieve the same result by using $set on a field, which is not included in the document.

Deleting data

As you have just seen, the update operator is quite flexible and allows trimming or pushing keys to your collections. If you need to delete a whole set of documents, then you can use the remove operator. When used without any parameter, it is equivalent to the TRUNCATE command in SQL terms:

```
> db.users.remove()
```

Most of the time, you need to be more selective when deleting documents as you might need to remove just a set of documents matching one or more conditions. For example, here is how to remove users older than 40:

```
> db.users.remove({ "age": { $gt: 40 } })
WriteResult({ "nRemoved" : 1 })
```

Just like the TRUNCATE statement in SQL, it just removes documents from a collection. If you want to delete the collection, then you need to use the drop() method, which deletes the whole collection structure, including any associated index:

```
> db.users.drop()
```

Beyond basic data types

Although the basic data types we have used so far will be fine for most use cases, there are a couple of additional types that are crucial to most applications, especially when mapping Mongo types to a language driver such as a Mongo driver for Java.

Arrays

MongoDB has a rich query language that supports storing and accessing documents as arrays. One of the great things about arrays in documents is that MongoDB understands their structure and knows how to reach inside arrays to perform operations on their content. This allows us to query on arrays and build indexes using their content.

Let's start creating a couple of documents containing an array of items:

```
> db.restaurant.insert({"menu" : ["bread", "pizza", "coke"]})
WriteResult({ "nInserted" : 1 })


> db.restaurant.insert({"menu" : ["bread", "omelette", "sprite"]})

WriteResult({ "nInserted" : 1 })
```

We will now show you how to query on the array selection to find the menu, which includes pizza:

```
> db.restaurant.find({"menu" : "pizza"})


{ "_id" : ObjectId("550abbfe89ef057ee0671650"), "menu" : [
"bread","pizza", "coke" ] }
```

Should you need to match arrays using more than one element, then you can use `$all`. This allows you to match a list of elements. For example, let's see how you can query on the above collection by matching two items in the menu:

```
> db.restaurant.find({"menu" : {$all : ["pizza", "coke"]}})

{ "_id" : ObjectId("550abbfe89ef057ee0671650"), "menu" : [ "bread",
"pizza", "coke" ] }
```

Embedded documents

You can use a document as a value for a key. This is called an embedded document. Embedded documents can be used to organize data in a more natural way than just a flat structure of key-value pairs. This matches well with most object-oriented languages, which holds a reference to another structure in their class.

Let's start by defining a structure, which is assigned to a variable in the mongo shell:

```
x = {
    "_id":1234,
    "owner":"Frank's Car",
    "cars":[
        {
            "year":2011,
            "model":"Ferrari",
            price:250000
        },
        {
            "year":2013,
            "model":"Porsche",
            price:250000
        }
    ]
}
```

Since the Mongo shell is a JavaScript interface, it is perfectly fine to write something like the preceding code and even use functions in order to enhance objects in the shell. Having defined our variable, we can insert it into the `cars` collection as follows:

```
> db.cars.insert(x);
WriteResult({ "nInserted" : 1 })
```

Alright. We have just inserted a document which in turn contains an array of documents. We can query our subdocument by using the dot notation. For example, we can choose the list of cars whose model is `Ferrari` by using the `cars.model` criteria:

```
> db.cars.find( { "cars.model": "Ferrari" }).pretty()
{
  "_id" : 1234,
  "owner" : "Frank's Car",
  "cars" : [
    {
      "year" : 2011,
      "model" : "Ferrari",
      "price" : 250000
    },
    {
      "year" : 2013,
      "model" : "Porsche",
      "price" : 250000
    }
  ]

}
```

 Also, the `pretty` function provides a pretty formatted JSON in the response.

Some useful functions

We will complete our excursus on the Mongo shell with some handy functions, which can be used to achieve a more precise control over your queries. The ones we will cover in this section are the `limit`, `sort`, and `skip` functions.

You can use the `limit` function to specify the maximum number of documents returned by your query. You obviously need to provide the number of records to be returned as a parameter. By setting this parameter to `0`, all the documents will be returned:

```
> db.users.find().limit(10)
```

The `sort` function, on the other hand, can be used to sort the results returned from the query in ascending (1) or descending (-1) order. This function is pretty much equivalent to the ORDER BY statement in SQL. Here is a basic example of `sort`:

```
> db.users.find({}).sort({"name":1})
```

```
{ "_id" : ObjectId("5506d5708d7bd8471669e674"), "name" : "francesco",
"age" : 44, "phone" : "123-456-789" }
{ "_id" : ObjectId("550ad3ef89ef057ee0671652"), "name" : "owen", "age" :
32, "phone" : "555-444-333" }
```

This example sorts the results based on the name key-value in ascending order, which is the default sorting order. If you want to switch to the descending order, then you would need to add the -1 flag to the `sort` operator.

> Note that the `sort` function when issued against the document's
> _id will be sorted on a time criteria.

The next one in the list is the `skip` function, which skips the first *n* documents in a collection. For example, here is how to skip the first document in a search across the `users` collection:

```
> db.users.find().skip(1)
{ "_id" : ObjectId("550ad3ef89ef057ee0671652"), "name" : "owen", "age" :
32, "phone" : "555-444-333" }
```

All the preceding commands can be also combined to produce a powerful expression. For example, the preceding command will return a different user when combined with a `sort` function in descending order:

```
> db.users.find().skip(1).sort({"name":-1})
{ "_id" : ObjectId("5506d5708d7bd8471669e674"), "name" : "francesco",
"age" : 44, "phone" : "123-456-789" }
```

Securing database access

We will conclude this chapter by informing you about database security. So far, we have started and used MongoDB without any authentication process. Actually, starting mongod without any additional option exposes the database to any user who is aware of the process.

We will show how to provide secure access by means of the mongo shell. So, launch the mongo shell and connect to the `admin` database, which holds information about the users:

```
use admin
```

Now, let's use the `createUser` function to add a user named `administrator` with the password `mypassword` and grant unlimited privileges (the role `root`):

```
db.createUser(
    {
       user: "administrator",
       pwd: "mypassword",
       roles: [ "root" ]
    }
)
```

Now, shut down the server by using the following command:

```
db.shutdownServer()
```

We will restart the database using the `--auth` option, which forces user authentication:

```
mongod --dbpath "C:\mongodb-win32-x86_64-3.0.3\data" --auth
```

Now, the database is started in secure mode. You can connect from the mongo shell in two different ways. The first one should be used with caution on Linux/Unix systems, as it exposes the user/password in the process list:

```
mongo -u administrator -p mypassword --authenticationDatabase admin
```

As an alternative, you can start the mongo shell and authenticate it at the beginning of the session (you need to select the admin database at first as the authentication keys are stored on the `admin` DB):

```
use admin
db.auth('admin','mypassword')

use yourdb
. . . .
```

Summary

This chapter has provided a whistle-stop tour of the basics of the MongoDB and NoSQL databases. We have gone through some advantages that can be gained when choosing a NoSQL database and the trade-offs compared with a relational database.

Then, we took you through the installation of MongoDB and some start up options that can be used to customize your server. Finally, we talked about the MongoDB shell and learned how to manipulate data using some basic CRUD operations.

In the next chapter, we will show you how to connect to MongoDB using the Java driver and perform some equivalent actions using Java.

2

Getting Started with Java Driver for MongoDB

This chapter discusses the MongoDB Java interface that consists of a JDBC driver that needs to be downloaded and included in your application's classpath. By using the MongoDB Java driver, you will be able to perform all the create/read/update/delete (CRUD) operations that we have so far accomplished using the mongo shell. The list of topics covered includes the following:

- Downloading and installing the MongoDB JDBC driver
- Setting up a basic Java project using Eclipse
- Performing common CRUD operations using a Java application

Getting the Mongo JDBC driver

The MongoDB Java driver can be downloaded from the Maven central repository at `http://central.maven.org/maven2/org/mongodb/mongo-java-driver/`. Make sure you download the latest stable release of it.

>
> At the time of writing, version 3.0.0 of the MongoDB Java driver has just been released. The new version of the driver deprecates some of the core interfaces available in version 2.*X*, which is still the de facto standard in Java projects using MongoDB. For this reason, we will start with the latest stable 2.*X* version, showing the new driver in action in the *Using the MongoDB Java driver version 3* section.

Once downloaded, you need to include it in your application classpath. As for every external library, you can add it to the classpath by using the `-classpath` option on the command line. For example:

```
-classpath mongo-java-driver-2.13.0.jar YourApplication.java
```

Creating your first project

Developing Java applications can be done in a variety of options. In a nutshell, you would need a development environment and the required libraries to compile and run your project. Most Java developers approach the development in two ways:

- Create a standalone Java project and include the required libraries in it. This is the simplest solution and could be used if you are developing a standalone Java application.

- Create a project using a framework like Maven or Gradle, which can help you define the project dependencies and assist you in the project setup and build management. This approach requires you to invest some time learning these frameworks; nevertheless, it pays big dividends if you are engineering enterprise applications that have lots of dependencies on external libraries. We will discuss Maven in *Chapter 4, MongoDB in the Java EE 7 Enterprise Environment*.

Both approaches require you to first download a development environment. We will use NetBeans 8.0.2 for this purpose, which can be downloaded from `https://netbeans.org/downloads/`.

Installing NetBeans is pretty simple; all you have to do is execute the installer (`netbeans-8.0.2-javaee-windows.exe` or `netbeans-8.0.2-javaee-windows.sh` for Linux). This will start a guided installation procedure requiring you to specify the installation path.

Creating a new Java project

The following steps will take you through the creation of a new Java project:

1. Start NetBeans and from the **File** menu, select **New Project**. Choose **Java Application** as displayed in the following window:

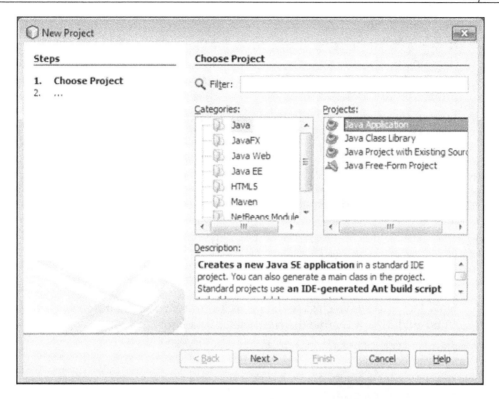

2. Enter a name for the project and choose a project location. Check the **Create Main Class** checkbox, so that you already have a skeleton Java class named `com.packtpub.mongo.chapter2.HelloMongo`, as shown in the following screenshot:

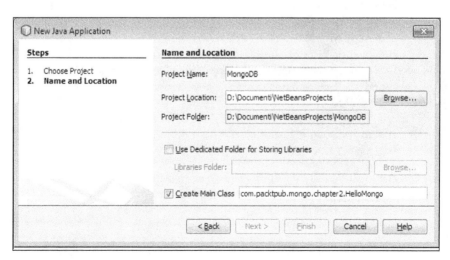

3. Click on **Finish**.

4. Now we will include the JDBC Driver for MongoDB in the project. Right-click on your project's **Libraries** folder and select **Add Jar/Folder**. From there, locate the `mongo-java-driver-2.13.0.jar`. At the end of this step, your project should look like this:

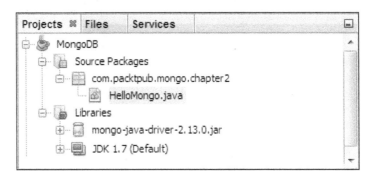

5. Now let's add a Java class to the project. From the **File** menu, select **Java Class** under **New**. Name the class as `HelloMongo`:

```java
package com.packtpub.mongo.chapter2;

import com.mongodb.DB;
import com.mongodb.MongoClient;

public class HelloMongo{

    private final static String  HOST  = "localhost";
    private final static int PORT = 27017;

    public static void main( String args[] ){
      try{
        // Connect to mongodb server on localhost
        MongoClient mongoClient = new MongoClient(HOST,
          PORT);

        DB db = mongoClient.getDB( "test" );


        System.out.println("Successfully connected to
          MongoDB");

      }
      catch(Exception e){
```

```
    System.err.println( e.getClass().getName() + ": " +
      e.getMessage() );
   }
  }
}
```

The preceding example is a quintessential Java example that connects to the test MongoDB running on the localhost on the default port (27017).

 The `com.mongodb.MongoClient` class represents your Java connection to the MongoDB database. For most applications, you should have one MongoClient instance for the entire JVM.

6. Next, the `com.Mongodb.DB` class provides a logical view of the database and can be used to retrieve a specific collection. As for the mongo shell, if the collection does not exist, it is created.

7. Run the application by right-clicking on the class and executing the **Java** application under **Run As**. On the Eclipse console, you should see the message **Successfully connected to MongoDB**.

Handling authentication

The above example will connect to an unsecured database. Although, this can be fine for your first examples, it is essential that you learn how to handle security in your Java code.

If you managed to create the administrator in *Chapter 1, Introduction to MongoDB,* now you can connect to a secured MongoDB database by using the credentials `administrator`/`mypassword` that we created earlier:

```
package com.packtpub.mongo.chapter2;

import java.util.Arrays;
import com.mongodb.DB;
import com.mongodb.MongoClient;
import com.mongodb.MongoCredential;
import com.mongodb.ServerAddress;

public class HelloSecureMongo{

  public static void main( String args[] ){
    try{
```

```
        MongoCredential credential =
          MongoCredential.createCredential("administrator",
            "admin", "mypassword".toCharArray());

        MongoClient mongoClient = new MongoClient(new
          ServerAddress("localhost"), Arrays.asList(credential));

        DB db = mongoClient.getDB( "test" );

        System.out.println("Successfully connected to secure
          database");
      }
    catch(Exception e){
      System.err.println( e.getClass().getName() + ": " +
        e.getMessage() );
    }
  }
}
```

The class that is responsible for the authentication, using release 2.13 or later, is `com.mongodb.MongoCredential`. This class represents the credentials (`administrator` in our case) used to authenticate against a Mongo database (named `admin`), as well as the source of the credentials and the authentication mechanism to use.

Execute the main class and expect the following output on the console:

Successfully connected to secure database

Inserting a document

So far, we have only tested the connectivity to the database. Now it's time to insert some documents and verify that the database contains them. The main class used by the Java driver for MongoDB (versions 2.X) for mapping Mongo objects is `com.mongodb.BasicDBObject`. You can use its fluent API to create Java representations of Mongo key-values by appending them to the object. In the following example, we create our first document in the `javastuff` collection. From the **File** menu, add a new **Java Class** named `com.packtpub.mongo.chapter2.SampleInsert`. The class will contain the following code:

```
package com.packtpub.mongo.chapter2;

import com.mongodb.BasicDBObject;
import com.mongodb.DBObject;
import com.mongodb.DB;
import com.mongodb.DBCollection;
```

```
import com.mongodb.MongoClient;


public class SampleInsert{

  private final static String  HOST  = "localhost";
  private final static int PORT = 27017;


  public static void main( String args[]  ){
    try{

      MongoClient mongoClient = new MongoClient(HOST,PORT );

      DB db = mongoClient.getDB( "sampledb" );

      DBCollection coll = db.getCollection("javastuff");
      DBObject doc = new BasicDBObject("name","owen")
      .append("age", 47)
      .append("email", "owen@mail.com")
      .append("phone", "111-222-333");

      coll.insert(doc);

    }
    catch(Exception e){
      System.err.println( e.getClass().getName() + ": " +
        e.getMessage() );
    }
  }
}
```

 Just like we did with the mongo shell, the insert method of the class com.mongodb.DBCollection also creates a collection automatically if it does not exist.

Run the preceding example and from the mongo shell, check whether the document has been added:

> **use sampledb**

> **db.javastuff.find().pretty()**

{

```
        "_id" : ObjectId("5513edcc3efba51b04574d5a"),

        "name" : "owen",

        "age" : 47,

        "email" : "owen@mail.com",

        "phone" : "111-222-333"

}
```

Creating embedded documents

The preceding example uses a flat data structure. Most of the time, you will have to deal with more complex types. For example, let's say that the user's information has to be stored in an embedded document. Luckily, creating this structure is intuitive, as you have to append a new instance of the document to the DBObject interface.

Let's see how to change the core section of the SampleInsert class:

```
DBObject doc = new BasicDBObject("name","frank")
  .append("age", 31)
  .append("info", new BasicDBObject("email",
    "frank@mail.com").append("phone", "222-111-444"));
```

Here is the structure that has been created on the database, which uses the info key to store some private information:

```
> db.javastuff.find({"name":"frank"}).pretty()
{
  "_id" : ObjectId("5513f1bd6c0d4cd4201ac006"),
  "name" : "frank",
  "age" : 31,
  "info" : {
  "email" : "frank@mail.com",
  "phone" : "222-111-444"
  }
}
```

Inserting an array of data

Another scenario could be creating arrays of data in your document. Again, the solution is pretty intuitive and uses the well known java.util.List class, which can be populated with a set of BasicDBObject. Each BasicDBObject class, in turn, contains the array of keys and values.

See the following example, which adds an array of kids to the user named john:

```java
public class ArrayInsert {

    private final static String  HOST  = "localhost";
    private final static int PORT = 27017;


    public static void main(String args[]) {
      try {
        MongoClient mongoClient = new MongoClient(HOST, PORT);

        DB db = mongoClient.getDB("sampledb");

        DBCollection coll = db.getCollection("javastuff");

        List<DBObject> kids = new ArrayList<>();
        kids.add(new BasicDBObject("name", "mike"));
        kids.add(new BasicDBObject("name", "faye"));

        DBObject doc = new BasicDBObject("name", "john")
          .append("age", 35)
          .append("kids", kids)
          .append("info",
            new BasicDBObject("email", "john@mail.com")
          .append("phone", "876-134-667"));
        coll.insert(doc);

      } catch (Exception e) {
        System.err.println(e.getClass().getName() + ": " +
          e.getMessage());
      }
    }
}
```

Execute the Java class. Now switch to the mongo shell and meet John's family:

```
> db.javastuff.find({"name":"john"}).pretty()
{
  "_id" : ObjectId("5513f8836c0df1301685315b"),
  "name" : "john",
  "age" : 35,
  "kids" : [
    {
```

```
      "name" : "mike"
    },
    {
      "name" : "faye"
    }
  ],
  "info" : {
    "email" : "john@mail.com",
    "phone" : "876-134-667"
  }
}
```

Using your own ID in documents

In the documents created so far, we have not used any unique identifier as the key. You should be aware that MongoDB by itself adds a _id identifier to your documents, which needs to be unique in all documents.

 The advantage of using the self-generated _id identifier is that it begins with a 4-byte value representing the seconds since the Unix epoch. Hence, you can sort documents on a time base by using the _id field.

In some cases, however, you might be prone to provide yourself the identifiers and use them to search through the documents.

Using your own identifiers is just a matter of setting the _id key within the com. mongodb.BasicDBObject structure. This way, MongoDB will not attempt to create its own keys. See the following snippet, which provides the _id that has the value 12345678:

```
DBCollection coll = db.getCollection("javastuff");

DBObject doc = new BasicDBObject("_id", "12345678")
    .append("name","jim")
    .append("age", 47)
    .append("info", new BasicDBObject("email",    "owen@mail.com").
append("phone", "111-222-333"));

coll.insert(doc);
```

Check from the console whether the ID has been assigned correctly:

```
> db.javastuff.find({"name": "jim"}).pretty()
{
        "_id" : "12345678",
        "name" : "jim",
        "age" : 47,
        "info" : {
                "email" : "jim@mail.com",
                "phone" : "111-222-333"
        }
}
```

Be careful when using your own IDs!

When providing your own keys, it is entirely your responsibility to care for duplicate key issues. Generally speaking, MongoDB documents can share the same keys; that's not true for the _id key, resulting in an exception if you try to insert two documents with the same _id:

```
com.mongodb.MongoException$DuplicateKey: {
"serverUsed" : "localhost:27017" , "ok" : 1 , "n" : 0
, "err" : "insertDocument :: caused by :: 11000 E11000
duplicate key error index: sampledb.javastuff.$_id_
dup key: { : \"12345678\" }" , "code" : 11000}
```

Querying data

We will now see how to use the Java API to query for your documents. Querying for documents with MongoDB resembles JDBC queries; the main difference is that the returned object is a `com.mongodb.DBCursor` class, which is an iterator over the database result.

In the following example, we are iterating over the `javastuff` collection that should contain the documents inserted so far:

```
package com.packtpub.mongo.chapter2;

import com.mongodb.DB;
import com.mongodb.DBCollection;
import com.mongodb.DBCursor;
import com.mongodb.DBObject;
import com.mongodb.MongoClient;
```

```
public class SampleQuery{

   private final static String  HOST  = "localhost";
   private final static int PORT = 27017;

   public static void main( String args[] ){
     try{
       MongoClient mongoClient = new MongoClient( HOST,PORT );

       DB db = mongoClient.getDB( "sampledb" );

       DBCollection coll = db.getCollection("javastuff");
       DBCursor cursor = coll.find();
       try {
         while(cursor.hasNext()) {
           DBObject object = cursor.next();
           System.out.println(object);
         }
       }
       finally {
         cursor.close();
       }

     }
     catch(Exception e) {
       System.err.println( e.getClass().getName() + ": " +
         e.getMessage() );
     }
   }
}
```

Depending on the documents you have inserted, the output could be something like this:

```
{ "_id" : { "$oid" : "5513f8836c0df1301685315b"} , "name" : "john" ,
"age" : 35 , "kids" : [ { "name" : "mike"} , { "name" : "faye"}] ,
"info" : { "email" : "john@mail.com" , "phone" : "876-134-667"}}
```

. . . .

Restricting the search to the first document

The `find` operator executed without any parameter returns the full cursor of a collection; pretty much like the `SELECT *` query in relational DB terms. If you are interested in reading just the first document in the collection, you could use the `findOne()` operation to get the first document in the collection. This method returns a single document (instead of the DBCursor that the `find()` operation returns). As you can see, the `findOne()` operator directly returns a `DBObject` instead of a `com.mongodb.DBCursor` class:

```
DBObject myDoc = coll.findOne();
System.out.println(myDoc);
```

Querying the number of documents in a collection

Another typical construct that you probably know from the SQL is the `SELECT count(*)` query that is useful to retrieve the number of records in a table. In MongoDB terms, you can get this value simply by invoking the `getCount` against a `DBCollection` class:

```
DBCollection coll = db.getCollection("javastuff");
System.out.println(coll.getCount());
```

As an alternative, you could execute the `count()` method over the `DBCursor` object:

```
DBCursor cursor = coll.find();
System.out.println(cursor.count());
```

Eager fetching of data using DBCursor

When `find` is executed and a DBCursor is executed you have a pointer to a database document. This means that the documents are fetched in the memory as you call `next()` method on the DBCursor.

On the other hand, you can eagerly load all the data into the memory by executing the `toArray()` method, which returns a `java.util.List` structure:

```
List list = collection.find( query ).toArray();
```

The problem with this approach is that you could potentially fill up the memory with lots of documents, which are eagerly loaded. You are therefore advised to include some operators such as `skip()` and `limit()` to control the amount of data to be loaded into the memory:

```
List list = collection.find( query ).skip( 100 ).
    limit( 10 ).toArray();
```

Just like you learned from the mongo shell, the `skip` operator can be used as an initial offset of your cursor whilst the `limit` construct can eventually load the first *n* occurrences in the cursor.

Filtering through the records

Typically, you will not need to fetch the whole set of documents in a collection. So, just like SQL uses WHERE conditions to filter records, in MongoDB you can restrict searches by creating a `BasicDBObject` and passing it to the `find` function as an argument. See the following example:

```
DBCollection coll = db.getCollection("javastuff");

DBObject query = new BasicDBObject("name", "owen");

DBCursor cursor = coll.find(query);

try {
    while(cursor.hasNext()) {
        System.out.println(cursor.next());
    }
} finally {
    cursor.close();
}
```

In the preceding example, we retrieve the documents in the `javastuff` collection, whose name key equals to `owen`. That's the equivalent of an SQL query like this:

```
SELECT * FROM javastuff WHERE name='owen'
```

Building more complex searches

As your collections keep growing, you will need to be more selective with your searches. For example, you could include multiple keys in your `BasicDBObject` that will eventually be passed to `find`. Recall the *Using ranges in your queries* section that you learned in *Chapter 1, Introduction to MongoDB*. We can then apply the same functions in our queries. For example, here is how to find documents whose name does not equal (`$ne`) to `Frank` and whose age is greater than `10`:

```
DBCollection coll = db.getCollection("javastuff");

DBObject query = new
        BasicDBObject("name", new BasicDBObject("$ne",
            "frank")).append("age", new BasicDBObject("$gt", 10));

DBCursor cursor = coll.find(query);
```

Updating documents

Having learned about create and read, we are half way through our CRUD track. The next operation you will learn is update. The DBCollection class contains an update method that can be used for this purpose. Let's say we have the following document:

```
> db.javastuff.find({"name":"frank"}).pretty()
{
  "_id" : ObjectId("55142c27627b27560bd365b1"),
  "name" : "frank",
  "age" : 31,
  "info" : {
  "email" : "frank@mail.com",
  "phone" : "222-111-444"
  }
}
```

Now we want to change the age value for this document by setting it to 23:

```
DBCollection coll = db.getCollection("javastuff");

DBObject newDocument = new BasicDBObject();
newDocument.put("age", 23);

DBObject searchQuery = new BasicDBObject().append("name", "owen");

coll.update(searchQuery, newDocument);
```

You might think that would do the trick, but wait! Let's have a look at our document using the mongo shell:

```
> db.javastuff.find({"age":23}).pretty()
```

```
{ "_id" : ObjectId("55142c27627b27560bd365b1"), "age" : 23 }
```

As you can see, the update statement has replaced the original document with another one, including only the keys and values we have passed to the update. In most cases, this is not what we want to achieve. If we want to update a particular value, we have to use the $set update modifier that we have already studied in the first chapter of this book:

```
DBCollection coll = db.getCollection("javastuff");

BasicDBObject newDocument = new BasicDBObject();
```

```
newDocument.append("$set", new BasicDBObject().append("age",
    23));

BasicDBObject searchQuery = new BasicDBObject().append("name",
"frank");

coll.update(searchQuery, newDocument);
```

So, suppose we restored the initial document with all the fields, this is the outcome of the update using the $set update modifier:

```
> db.javastuff.find({"age":23}).pretty()
{
  "_id" : ObjectId("5514326e627b383428c2ccd8"),
  "name" : "frank",
  "age" : 23,
  "in,fo" : {
    "email" : "frank@mail.com",
    "phone" : "222-111-444"
  }
}
```

Please note that the DBCollection class overloads the method update with update(DBObject q, DBObject o, boolean upsert, boolean multi). The first parameter (upsert) determines whether the database should create the element if it does not exist. The second one (multi) causes the update to be applied to all matching objects.

Deleting documents

The operator to be used for deleting documents is obviously delete. As for other operators, it includes several variants. In its simplest form, when executed over a single document returned, it will remove it:

```
MongoClient mongoClient = new MongoClient("localhost", 27017);

DB db = mongoClient.getDB("sampledb");
DBCollection coll = db.getCollection("javastuff");
DBObject doc = coll.findOne();

coll.remove(doc);
```

Most of the time you will need to filter the documents to be deleted. Here is how to delete the document with the key `frank`:

```
DBObject document = new BasicDBObject();
document.put("name", "frank");

coll.remove(document);
```

Deleting a set of documents

Bulk deletion of documents can be achieved by including the keys in a `List` and building an `$in` modifier expression that uses this list. Let's see, for example, how to delete all records whose age ranges from 0 to 49:

```
BasicDBObject deleteQuery = new BasicDBObject();
List<Integer> list = new ArrayList<Integer>();

for (int i=0;i<50;i++)
list.add(i);

deleteQuery.put("age", new BasicDBObject("$in", list));
coll.remove(deleteQuery);
```

Performing operations on collections

By using the Java driver, you are also able to manipulate the collection objects, which are the equivalent of database tables. And you should be fully aware that if you attempt to retrieve a nonexistent collection and insert a document into it, the collection will be automatically created by MongoDB:

```
DBCollection coll = db.getCollection("mycol");

DBObject doc = new BasicDBObject("name","owen")
.append("age", 47)
.append("email", "owen@mail.com").append("phone", "111-222-333");

coll.insert(doc);

System.out.println("Collection mycol successfully created");
```

You can also explicitly create a collection by means of Capped collections.

 A Capped collection is a fixed-size collection, which supports high-throughput insert/retrieve operations based on insertion order. A capped collection acts much the same as a circular buffer. As a collection fills out its allocated space, it overwrites the oldest documents to make room.

In order to create a Capped collection from the Java driver, you need to pass a set of options along with the collection name, which include:

- The max argument, which specifies the maximum number of documents allowed in the collection.

- The size argument, which specifies the size of the capped collection in bytes. This argument is always required, even when you specify the maximum number of documents.

Here is, for example, how to create a capped collection named orderedcollection, which has a size of 1000000000 bytes:

```
DBObject options = BasicDBObjectBuilder.start().add("capped",
  true).add("size", 10000000001).get();

DBCollection  collection =
  db.createCollection("orderedcollection", options);
```

Listing collections

The list of collections is available as a set of strings by invoking getCollectionNames over the com.mongodb.DB class. Here is a quick snippet that does exactly this:

```
for (String s : db.getCollectionNames()) {
  System.out.println(s);
}
```

That should output the available collections, which, in our case, are:

```
cars
javastuff
orderedcollectioon
system.indexes
```

Perhaps, you have noticed the system.indexes collection. This is a special kind of collection containing the list of indexes available in the collection. More details about indexes are discussed in the next chapter.

Dropping a collection

The drop operator can also be used to delete a collection of data. This operation is pretty equivalent to the DROP TABLE query that is executed in SQL. Here is how to use the drop operator to drop the collection named testCollection:

```
DBCollection coll = db.getCollection("testCollection");
coll.drop();
```

On the other hand, if you need to delete all the documents in a collection (just like a TRUNCATE would do in a RDBMS), then you have to iterate over the documents in the collection and delete them individually:

```
DBCursor c = collection.find();
  while (c.hasNext()) {
    collection.remove(c.next());
  }
```

Using the MongoDB Java driver version 3

While this book is being written, a new major version of the Java driver has just been released. This version is number 3 and can be downloaded just like version 2 from http://central.maven.org/maven2/org/mongodb/mongo-java-driver.

As the core classes and interfaces used by the new API are different compared to the 2.X version, you will have to choose which Mongo Java driver (http://central.maven.org/maven2/org/mongodb/mongo-java-driver) is fit for your projects. This decision might not be that simple, as each version has some advantages. In particular:

- Developing applications with the Java driver for MongoDB 3 can be more intuitive, typesafe, and run faster as it deals with a document schema that is translated in BSON

- Developing applications with the Java driver for MongoDB 2, on the other hand, has a rich community of users, and it is generally adopted in many frameworks that have some kind of interaction with MongoDB from Java

Running the HelloWorld class with driver v.3

The first evident change in the MongoDB Java API is that the `com.mongodb.DB` class has been deprecated in favor of the import `com.mongodb.client.MongoDatabase`, which is a major improvement in the driver API featuring a thread-safe interface towards the databases on MongoDB.

Here is the `HelloWorld` class written with the new API:

```
package com.packtpub.mongo.chapter2;

import com.mongodb.MongoClient;
import com.mongodb.client.MongoDatabase;
import com.mongodb.client.MongoIterable;


public class HelloMongo{
  private final static String  HOST  = "localhost";
  private final static int PORT = 27017;

  public static void main( String args[] ){
    try{
      MongoClient mongoClient = new MongoClient( HOST , PORT );
      // Now connect to the test database
      MongoDatabase db = mongoClient.getDatabase("test");
      System.out.println("Connect to database successfully ");

    }
    catch(Exception e){
      System.err.println( e.getClass().getName() + ": " +
        e.getMessage() );
    }
  }
}
```

Be sure to include the new driver in your project's library. As usual, run the project by clicking on **Class** and selecting **Run File**. Once executed, you should expect to read the following message on your Java console:

```
Connect to database successfully
```

Managing collections

Collections are created using the driver version 3 in much the same way as the older driver. The main difference is that the provider of collections is now the interface `com.mongodb.client.MongoDatabase`. You will have to use the `createCollection` method of the `MongoDatabase` class as follows:

```
db.createCollection("collection1");
```

In order to browse through the list of collections, you can use the `listCollectionNames` method of the `MongoDatabase` class, which returns a `com.mongodb.client.MongoIterable` object:

```
MongoIterable<String> collections = db.listCollectionNames();
MongoCursor<String> cursor = collections.iterator();
while (cursor.hasNext()) {
System.out.println(cursor.next());
}
```

 MongoIterable is the result from an operation, such as a query.

Finally, in order to connect to a specific collection and start working with it, you can use the method `getCollection`, passing the name of the collection as a parameter:

```
MongoCollection col = db.getCollection("users");
```

Inserting data into the database

The most marked difference between the driver versions is the class used to map the documents. The driver version 3 uses a new class named `org.bson.Document` to create the document on the database. Let's see a practical example of this, we will insert the following document:

```
{"name" : "john",
"age" : 25,
"phone":"321-654-987"
}
```

To do this, we can, at first, retrieve the collection we want to use by using the method `getCollection` that we have just learned.

Next, we will be using the `org.bson.Document` class to create the document and then just simply insert it into the collection using the `insertOne()` method.

Here is the full source code of it:

```java
package com.packtpub.mongo.chapter2;

import org.bson.Document;
import com.mongodb.MongoClient;
import com.mongodb.client.MongoCollection;
import com.mongodb.client.MongoDatabase;


public class InsertMongo {

  private final static String  HOST  = "localhost";
  private final static int PORT = 27017;

  public static void main(String args[]) {
    try {
      MongoClient mongoClient = new MongoClient(HOST, PORT);

      MongoDatabase db = mongoClient.getDatabase("sampledb");
      MongoCollection<Document> coll = db.getCollection("users");

      Document doc = new Document("name", "john").append("age",
        25)  .append("phone", "321-654-987");
      coll.insertOne(doc);

    }
    catch (Exception e) {
      System.err.println(e.getClass().getName() + ": " +
        e.getMessage());
    }
  }
}
```

Inserting embedded documents

The above document is a very basic one. Let's see how to insert a more complex document like the following one that contains an embedded document:

```
{
  "name" : "louis",
  "age" : 29,
  "info" : {
    email : "louis@mail.com",
```

```
    phone : "876-134-667"
    }
}
```

In terms of Java code, there is a perfect match with the document structure as we will embed a new document within the existing one:

```
Document doc = new Document("name", "louis").append("age", 29)
  .append("info",
    new Document("email", "louis@mail.com").append(
    "phone", "876-134-667"));


coll.insertOne(doc);
```

Inserting multiple documents

In the first example, we have used the `insertOne` method to insert a single document into MongoDB. If you need to insert multiple documents from a single point, then you can store your documents in `java.util.List` and pass it as an argument to the `insertMany` method of your collection:

```
List<Document> documents = new ArrayList<Document>();
for (int i = 0; i < 10; i++) {
  documents.add(new Document("key", UUID.randomUUID().toString()));
}
coll.insertMany(documents);
```

Querying documents

A new interface named `com.mongodb.client.MongoCursor` has been added to iterate over the list of documents that is queried. The behavior is quite the same compared to the `com.mongodb.DBCursor` class available in the driver version 2, the only difference is that it is now iterating over a list of document objects:

```
MongoCollection<Document> coll = db.getCollection("users");


MongoCursor<Document> cursor = coll.find().iterator();
try {
  while (cursor.hasNext()) {
      Document doc = cursor.next();

      System.out.println(doc.toJson());
  }
```

```
} finally {
  cursor.close();
}
```

 Please notice the toJson method, which is a convenience method that can be used to output the document into the JSON format.

Filtering through documents

Filtering documents using the driver version 3 can now be performed using compile-safe methods thanks to the com.mongodb.client.model.Filters class. This class contains a set of static imports that are able to match the most common querying criteria.

For example, here is a sample class that queries documents, whose name equals to john:

```
package com.packtpub.mongo.chapter2;

import com.mongodb.MongoClient;
import com.mongodb.client.MongoCollection;
import com.mongodb.client.MongoCursor;
import com.mongodb.client.MongoDatabase;
import static com.mongodb.client.model.Filters.eq;
import org.bson.Document;

public class MongoFilter {

  private final static String HOST = "localhost";
  private final static int PORT = 27017;

  public static void main(String args[]) {
    try {

      MongoClient mongoClient = new MongoClient(HOST, PORT);

      MongoDatabase db = mongoClient.getDatabase("sampledb");
      MongoCollection<Document> coll = db.getCollection("users");

      Document newDoc = new Document("name", "john").append("age",
        25).append("phone", "321-654-987");
      coll.insertOne(newDoc);
```

```
MongoCursor<Document> cursor = coll.find(eq("name",
  "john")).iterator();

try {
  while (cursor.hasNext()) {
    Document doc = cursor.next();

    System.out.println(doc.toJson());
  }
} finally {
  cursor.close();
}

} catch (Exception e) {
System.err.println(e.getClass().getName() + ": " +
  e.getMessage());
}
}
}
```

Filters can also be combined with multiple conditions. For example, here is how to retrieve the users who are aged between 21 and 40:

```
MongoCursor<Document> cursor = collection.find(and(gt("age", 20),
  lte("age", 40))).iterator();
```

On the other hand, if you want to retrieve only the first document from the list, then the `first()` method is your choice:

```
Document myDoc = coll.find(eq("name", "john")).first();
```

The full list of available filters is pretty lengthy; however, you can keep this link as a reference `http://api.mongodb.org/java/3.0/com/mongodb/client/model/Filters.html`.

Updating documents

In order to update a document, you can use two methods of the `MongoCollection` class; `updateOne` is a simple construct to update a single document of a collection. For example, here is how you set the key `age` to `50` for the first key whose name is `john`:

```
MongoCollection<org.bson.Document> coll =
  db.getCollection("users");
coll.updateOne(eq("name", "john"), new Document("$set", new
  Document("age", 50)));
```

The preceding method updates just a single document, that is the first one matching the preceding filter (whose name equals to `john`). In case you want to apply the update to all occurrences of the same condition, you can use the `updateMany` method, which returns an instance of `com.mongodb.client.result.UpdateResult`:

```
UpdateResult updateResult = coll.updateMany(eq("name", "john"),
    new Document("$set", new Document("age", 50)));
```

The update count is available through `getModifiedCount()` as follows:

```
System.out.println(updateResult.getModifiedCount());
```

Deleting documents

`MongoCollection` also contains methods for removing documents from a collection. The corresponding methods are `deleteOne` and `deleteMany`. The former can be used to delete the first record matching a key:

```
MongoCollection<org.bson.Document> coll =
    db.getCollection("users");
coll.deleteOne(eq("name", "john"));
```

Here is the `deleteMany` method that deletes all the users whose names are `john`:

```
DeleteResult deleteResult = coll.deleteMany(eq("name", "john"));

System.out.println(deleteResult.getDeletedCount());
```

Summary

In this chapter, we covered the first steps with MongoDB and the Java driver, which allows you to perform the same operations that are available in the mongo shell, which was covered in the previous chapter.

As there are two main versions of the MongoDB driver (2.X and 3.X), we have covered the basics of both APIs so that you can decide to code your applications using a consolidated API (2.X) or pilot them towards the newer 3.X API.

The next chapter is going to teach you some more advanced topics about the Java driver such as Java to JSON mapping using the Google Gson API, using indexes, and more.

3
MongoDB CRUD
Beyond the Basics

The previous chapter of this book took you through the first green bar in connecting Java and MongoDB. You learned how to perform some basic create, read, update, and delete operations using simple Java classes. It is now time to address some advanced concerns, which are part of every real work application. Here is what we are going to discuss in this chapter in detail:

- How to map MongoDB documents in Java objects and vice versa
- How to apply indexes to your documents to speed up searches
- How to code bulk operations to improve the speed of your insert/updates

Seeing MongoDB through the Java lens

So far, we have had some interaction with the Java driver using com.mongodb. DBObject as a simple translator between the Java objects and the MongoDB documents:

```
DBCursor cursor = coll.find();

try {
  while(cursor.hasNext()) {
    DBObject object = cursor.next();
    System.out.println(object.get("username"));
  }
} finally {
  cursor.close();
}
```

When you move from the basics to a more complex project, you will find that this approach requires writing lots of code and it is prone to runtime errors.

There are some solutions to this problem with different degrees of complexity. In this chapter, we will account for some simple ones that require a minimal learning curve. Later on, in *Chapter 5, Managing Data Persistence with MongoDB and JPA*, we will describe how to use some frameworks that can let you persist Java objects directly into MongoDB as documents, at the price of some enhanced complexity.

Here is what we are going to learn in the next section:

- Extending the MongoDB core classes to save custom objects into the database.
- Using a Java library to translate Mongo documents into Java objects (and vice versa) via JSON.

Extending the MongoDB core classes

The first approach requires that you either implement `com.mongodb.DBObject` (and provide some default implementation of its core methods) or directly extend `com.mongodb.BasicDBObject`.

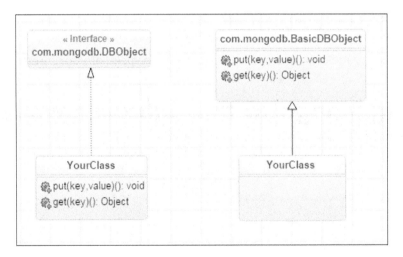

As you can see from the preceding diagram, the first choice is more flexible; however, you need to provide some default implementation for the basic methods of the collections mapped by your POJO. (For the sake of simplicity, only the two most common methods, **put** and **get**, are indicated in the diagram.)

Let's see a minimal implementation of a Java class `SimplePojo`, which implements
`com.mongodb.DBObject`:

```java
package com.packtpub.mongo.chapter3;

import java.util.HashMap;
import java.util.Map;
import java.util.Set;

import org.bson.BSONObject;

import com.mongodb.DBObject;


public class SimplePojo implements DBObject {
    private Map<String, Object> data;
    private boolean partial;

    public SimplePojo() {
        data = new HashMap<>();
        partial = false;
    }

    @Override
    public Object put(String key, Object value) {
        return data.put(key, value);
    }

    @SuppressWarnings("unchecked")
    @Override
    public void putAll(BSONObject o) {
        data.putAll(o.toMap());
    }

    @SuppressWarnings({ "rawtypes", "unchecked" })
    @Override
    public void putAll(Map m) {
        data.putAll(m);
    }

    @Override
    public Object get(String key) {
```

```java
        return data.get(key);
    }

    @SuppressWarnings("rawtypes")
    @Override
    public Map toMap() {
        return data;
    }

    @Override
    public Object removeField(String key) {
        return data.remove(key);
    }

    @Override
    public boolean containsKey(String key) {
        return data.containsKey(key);
    }

    @Override
    public boolean containsField(String key) {
        return data.containsKey(key);
    }

    @Override
    public Set<String> keySet() {
        return data.keySet();
    }

    @Override
    public void markAsPartialObject() {
        partial = true;
    }

    @Override
    public boolean isPartialObject() {
        return partial;
    }
}
```

As you can see, we had to provide a default implementation for the methods specified in the `com.mongodb.DBObject` interface. Now we'll insert our `SimplePojo` class directly into our collection, as follows:

```
DB db = mongoClient.getDB( "sampledb" );
DBCollection coll = db.getCollection("pojo");

SimplePojo obj = new SimplePojo();
obj.put("user", "user1");
obj.put("message", "message");
obj.put("date", new Date());

coll.insert(obj);
```

Retrieving the Java class from the database is straightforward as well. First you need to call `setObjectClass` on your collection to state that you are going to retrieve objects of that type. Then you can use the finder methods of the collection as usual:

```
coll.setObjectClass(SimplePojo.class);

SimplePojo tw = (SimplePojo)coll.findOne();

System.out.println(tw.get("user"));
```

The major downside of this approach is that you have to provide some boilerplate code with a default implementation of the `com.mongodb.DBObject` class. As an alternative, you can consider extending the class `com.mongodb.BasicDBObject`, which already contains a `com.mongodb.DBObject` default implementation. This will avoid writing boilerplate code, at the price of lack of flexibility in your code. As a matter of fact, you will not be able to extend any other class from your code.

Here is a rewritten version of `SimplePojo` that extends `com.mongodb.BasicDBObject` and merely contains a business method to return an uppercased version of a key requested:

```
package com.packtpub.mongo.chapter3;

import com.mongodb.BasicDBObject;

public class SimplePojo extends BasicDBObject {

  public String getUpperCaseKey(String key) {
    String value = (String) super.get(key);
    if (value != null)
      return value.toUpperCase();
```

```
    else
       return null;

   }
}
```

In terms of implementation, nothing will change, and you can pass your Java classes to the `insert` method of your collection, as you already know:

```
SimplePojo pojo = new SimplePojo();
pojo.put("user", "user2");
pojo.put("message", "msg");
pojo.put("date", new Date());

coll.insert(pojo);
```

Using the Gson API with MongoDB

Using JSON as a medium between Java and external system is a well-tested integration pattern. There are several libraries available to serialize and deserialize Java classes in JSON, the most popular one being Google's Gson (https://code. google.com/p/google-gson/). This API provides two simple `toJson()` and `fromJson()` constructs to convert Java objects to JSON and vice versa; besides this, Gson supports converting arbitrarily complex objects including deep inheritance hierarchies and makes extensive use of Java's generic types.

Downloading the Gson API

You can download the latest release of Gson from the Maven central repository at http://search.maven.org/#browse%7C472424538.

Include the JAR driver of Gson in the libraries of your project, as displayed in the following screenshot:

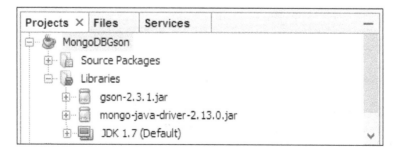

If you are using Maven, then you can include the following dependency in your `pom.xml` file (see the next chapter for more details about using Maven in your projects):

```xml
<dependency>
    <groupId>com.google.code.gson</groupId>
    <artifactId>gson</artifactId>
    <version>2.3.1</version>
</dependency>
```

Using Gson to map a MongoDB document

In the first example, we will map a MongoDB document with a Java class composed of a set of fields. So first, let's create a document that contains some basic keys:

```java
MongoClient mongoClient = new MongoClient("localhost", 27017);

DB db = mongoClient.getDB("sampledb");

DBCollection coll = db.getCollection("javastuff");

DBObject doc = new BasicDBObject("name", "owen")
  .append("age", 25)
  .append("email", "owen@gmail.com")
  .append("phone", "321-456-778");

coll.insert(doc);
```

As evident from the following document query, a document has been created in the `javastuff` collection:

```
> db.javastuff.find().pretty()
{
  "_id" : ObjectId("55266979d3d5368080f97f92"),
  "name" : "owen",
  "age" : 25,
  "email" : "owen@gmail.com",
  "phone" : "321-456-778"
}
```

Now let's create a simple Java bean that will be able to contain this document structure:

```java
public class Customer {

    String name;
```

```
    int age;
    String email;
    String phone;

    public Customer(String name, int age, String email, String
      phone) {
      super();
      this.name = name;
      this.age = age;
      this.email = email;
      this.phone = phone;
    }

    @Override
    public String toString() {
      return "Customer [name=" + name + ", age=" + age + ", email="
        + email  + ", phone=" + phone + "]";
    }
}
```

 Please note that it is not necessary to use any annotations to indicate that a class field is to be included for serialization and deserialization. By default, all fields contained in the class (and its superclasses) will be serialized into Java objects. In the *Custom field names in your Java classes* section, we will show you how to use annotations to map the field with custom names.

Being based on simple Java types such as string and int, mapping the MongoDB document to the Customer Java class is a piece of cake. Let's see how to do it:

```
Gson gson = new Gson();
DBObject doc = new BasicDBObject("name", "owen");

DBObject obj = coll.findOne(doc);
Customer c = gson.fromJson(obj.toString(), Customer.class);
System.out.println("Found customer " + c);
```

The expected output will be the toString() method of the Customer class that dumps the fields contained in the class:

```
Customer [name=owen, age=25, email=owen@gmail.com,
  phone=321-456-778]
```

Inserting Java objects as a document

The Google's Gson API can also leverage the reverse process, that is, inserting a Java class into MongoDB via JSON. The trick is done by the `toJson` method that serializes a Java class into the JSON format:

```
DB db = mongoClient.getDB("sampledb");

DBCollection coll = db.getCollection("javastuff");

System.out.println("Collection created successfully");

Customer c = new Customer("john", 22, "john@gmail.com",
    "777-666-555");

Gson gson = new Gson();
String json = gson.toJson(c);

DBObject dbObject = (DBObject) JSON.parse(json);

coll.insert(dbObject);
```

In the above example, the JSON string mapping the `Customer` class is stored in the string JSON. You can then use the static `parse` method of the `com.mongodb.util.JSON` class to convert the JSON string into a `DBObject` type.

The inserted structure will be as follows:

```
> db.javastuff.find({"name":"john"}).pretty()
{
        "_id" : ObjectId("55268359d3d51c80bdb231b5"),
        "name" : "john",
        "age" : 22,
        "email" : "john@gmail.com",
        "phone" : "777-666-555"

}
```

Mapping embedded documents

So far, we have mapped very simple basic structures with MongoDB. In real world cases, you will have to deal with Java classes having references to other objects. For example, we could think of a `Customer` class, which contains some information in a separate class named `Info`:

```java
package com.packtpub.chapter3.mongodemo;

public class CustomerInfo {

  String name;
  Info info;

  public CustomerInfo(String name, int age, String email, String
    phone) {

    this.name = name;

    this.info = new Info(age, email, phone);
  }

  public Info getInfo() {
    return info;
  }

  public void setInfo(Info info) {
    this.info = info;
  }

  public String getName() {
    return name;
  }

  public void setName(String name) {
    this.name = name;
  }

  @Override
  public String toString() {
    return "CustomerInfo [name=" + name + ", info=" + this.info +
      "] " ;
  }

  class Info {
```

```java
      public Info(int age, String email, String phone) {
        super();
        this.email = email;
        this.phone = phone;
        this.age = age;
      }
      public Info( ) {

      }
      String email;
      String phone;
      int age;

      public String getEmail() {
        return email;
      }

      public void setEmail(String email) {
        this.email = email;
      }

      public String getPhone() {
        return phone;
      }

      public void setPhone(String phone) {
        this.phone = phone;
      }

      public int getAge() {
        return age;
      }

      public void setAge(int age) {
        this.age = age;
      }

      @Override
      public String toString() {
        return "Info [email=" + email + ", phone=" + phone + ",
          age=" + age + "]";
      }

    }
  }
```

In the new class called `CustomerInfo`, we have highlighted the fields that will be mapped by MongoDB keys.

As you are aware, creating embedded documents in MongoDB can be done by setting a key to a `DBObject` structure containing the embedded document. In our case, we will structure the `info` key to contain the embedded document's information:

```
BasicDBObject doc = new BasicDBObject("name",
    "owen").append("info", new BasicDBObject("age",
      25).append("email", "owen@gmail.com").append("phone",
        "321-456-778"));

coll.insert(doc);

DBObject obj = coll.findOne(doc);

CustomerInfo c = gson.fromJson(obj.toString(),
    CustomerInfo.class);

System.out.println("Found customer " + c);
```

The expected output should match the following query executed through the mongo shell:

```
> db.javastuff.find({"name":"owen"}).pretty()
{
  "_id" : ObjectId("5526888bd3d56a86cea8ea12"),
  "name" : "owen",
  "info" : {
    "age" : 25,
    "email" : "owen@gmail.com",
    "phone" : "321-456-778"
  }
}
```

Custom field names in your Java classes

The `Customer` class contains a set of fields that are exactly equivalent to the key names to be found in the MongoDB collection. The schema of a MongoDB document is, however, quite flexible compared to a standard database table. One simple strategy could be choosing custom names for your class fields and mapping the corresponding MongoDB keys with the `com.google.gson.annotations.SerializedName` annotation. See the following class as an example:

```
import com.google.gson.annotations.SerializedName;

public class Customer {

    @SerializedName("name")
    String userName;

    @SerializedName("age")
    int userAge;

    @SerializedName("email")
    String userEmail;

    @SerializedName("phone")
    String userPhone;

}
```

In the next section, we will deal with a more complex concern, that is, mapping complex BSON types used by MongoDB to store entries.

Mapping complex BSON types

The preceding examples used simple Java types such as String and Integers. Sometimes, however, you might need to use a custom serialization/deserialization strategy for your classes.

For example, consider the following document structure:

```
{
    "_id" : ObjectId("5527b0bbd3d53064aac7c991"),
    "name" : "john",
    "age" : 22,
    "email" : "john@gmail.com",
    "phone" : "777-666-555"
}
```

You might think that adding the _id field to the Customer class will do the job of mapping Mongo's _id key:

```
public Customer(Object _id, String name, int age, String email,
    String phone) {
    super();
    this._id = _id;
    this.name = name;
    this.age = age;
```

```
        this.email = email;
        this.phone = phone;
    }
    public String toString() {
        return "Customer{" + "_id=" + _id + ", name=" + name + ", age="
            + age + ", email=" + email + ", phone=" + phone + '}';
    }
```

Let's see what happens if we try to deserialize the preceding document by using the fromJson method:

```
Customer c = gson.fromJson(obj.toString(), Customer.class);

System.out.println(c);
```

What we are trying to achieve is the following representation of the Customer class:

```
{_id=558c1007578ef44c4cbb0eb8, name=owen, age=25,
    email=owen@gmail.com, phone=321-456-778}
```

However, as you can see from the following output, the _id object was not correctly parsed as we expected:

```
_id={$oid=5527b117d3d511091e1735e2}, name=owen, age=22,
    email=john@gmail.com, phone=777-666-555
```

 Many other examples exist, for example, if you are dealing with date and time libraries.

Luckily, Gson allows registering custom serializers/deserializers so that you can convert these objects into the type that is needed by your application.

This is done in two steps:

1. At first you need to code a serializer (if you are inserting custom types in MongoDB) or a deserializer (if you are going to parse custom entries contained in MongoDB).

2. Then, you need to register this custom adapter.

Let's see both steps, in case you want to parse the _id unique identifier of MongoDB documents.

A custom deserializer needs to implement the com.google.gson. JsonDeserializer class as follows:

```
import com.google.gson.JsonDeserializationContext;
import com.google.gson.JsonDeserializer;
```

```java
import com.google.gson.JsonElement;
import com.google.gson.JsonObject;
import com.google.gson.JsonParseException;

public class CustomAdapter implements JsonDeserializer<Customer> {

  public Customer deserialize(JsonElement json,
    java.lang.reflect.Type typeOfT, JsonDeserializationContext
      context) throws JsonParseException {
    JsonObject jObj = json.getAsJsonObject();

    String id =
      jObj.get("_id").toString().replaceAll(".*\"(\\w+)\"}",
        "$1");

    String name = jObj.get("name") != null ?
      jObj.get("name").getAsString() : "";
    String email = jObj.get("email")!= null ?
      jObj.get("email").getAsString() : "";
    String phone = jObj.get("phone")!= null ?
      jObj.get("phone").getAsString() : "";
    int age = jObj.get("age")!= null ? jObj.get("age").getAsInt()
      : 0;

    return new Customer(id,name,age,email,phone);
  }
}
```

As you can see, this class contains the deserialization logic in the method deserialize, where each field is parsed according to your custom parsing rules. In this case, the value of the _id field is extracted using a regular expression, which scans for the identifier contained in the parentheses.

 Please note that using a schemaless database implies a lack of control over the data contained in your collection. As you can see, we had to check against null on each field of our document.

Some changes will also be required in your main Java class, so that you register the adapter on the Gson class, by means of the registerTypeAdapter method contained in the com.google.gson.GsonBuilder class:

```java
GsonBuilder builder=new GsonBuilder();

Gson gson = new GsonBuilder().registerTypeAdapter(Customer.class, new
CustomAdapter()).create();
```

```
BasicDBObject doc = new BasicDBObject("name", "owen");

DBObject obj = coll.findOne(doc);

Customer c = gson.fromJson(obj.toString(), Customer.class);
System.out.println("Found customer " + c);
```

Now the `toString` output of the `Customer` class reveals that you have been able to parse the `$id` field correctly:

```
_id=5527b117d3d511091e1735e2, name=owen, age=22,
  email=john@gmail.com, phone=777-666-555
```

Using indexes in your applications

The concept of an index in a database is pretty equivalent to the index contained in a book. So, instead of searching for a section across all the pages of the book onwards, you search for the relevant section in the index and then open the book on that page.

This concept has been adopted by all relational databases and it works quite the same on MongoDB, that is, by creating a special data structure that is able to store a small part of the collection's dataset in such a way that is easy to traverse from.

Without using indexes, MongoDB must perform an expensive collection scan, which means to scan every document in a collection, in order to find those documents that match the query string. Indexes can improve the efficiency of your queries by limiting the number of documents they must inspect on each query.

 This is not true in every case. As a matter of fact, a built-in index already exists on every collection on the _id field. This index is unique and prevents duplicate insertions using the _id field in a collection.

Let's see a practical example:

```
MongoClient mongoClient = new MongoClient("localhost", 27017);

DB db = mongoClient.getDB("sampledb");

DBCollection coll = db.getCollection("indextest");

for (int ii=0;ii<100000;ii++) {

DBObject doc = new BasicDBObject("userid", ii);
```

```
        coll.insert(doc);

    }
```

Here, we are inserting 1,00,000 documents in one go. Once the insertion completes, we can move to the mongo shell and execute the `explain` function to see what happens behind the scenes when mongo performs a query:

```
> db.indextest.find({userid: 50000}).explain("executionStats")
{
    "queryPlanner":{
        "plannerVersion":1,
        "namespace":"sampledb.indextest",
        "indexFilterSet":false,
        "parsedQuery":{
            "userid":{
                "$eq":"1111"
            }
        },
        "winningPlan":{
            "stage":"COLLSCAN",
            "filter":{
                "userid":{
                    "$eq":"1111"
                }
            },
            "direction":"forward"
        },
        "rejectedPlans":[
            ]
    },
    "executionStats":{
        "executionSuccess":true,
        "nReturned":0,
        "executionTimeMillis":6,
        "totalKeysExamined":0,
        "totalDocsExamined":100000,
        "executionStages":{
```

```
      "stage":"COLLSCAN",
      "filter":{
        "userid":{
          "$eq":"1111"
        }
      },
      "nReturned":0,
      "executionTimeMillisEstimate":0,
      "works":10002,
      "advanced":0,
      "needTime":10001,
      "needFetch":0,
      "saveState":78,
      "restoreState":78,
      "isEOF":1,
      "invalidates":0,
      "direction":"forward",
      "docsExamined":100000
    },
    "allPlansExecution":[

    ]
  },
  "serverInfo":{

    . . . .

  }
}
```

The `totalDocsExamined` attribute reveals the number of documents MongoDB has looked through; as you can see, every single document has been searched. Although the time needed to scan the collection might look insignificant (6 ms) this is due to the fact that we are dealing with a minimal document and that of course MongoDB is quite fast!

Also, the attribute `totalKeysExamined` set to `0` indicates that no index key was scanned during the search.

Besides this, you might instruct the Mongo cursor to stop looking through other documents once an occurrence is found using the `limit(1)` operator (which is also available through the Java driver). That could be helpful but may not be exactly what you are looking for in your search.

In the next section, we will see how to use an index to limit the number of documents to be scanned.

Defining an index in your Java classes

Adding an index to your collection is quite easy. In order to do that, you need to specify which fields of a document need to be indexed and state whether the index ordering is going to be in ascending (1) or descending (-1) order. For example, the following creates an ascending index on the `userid` field:

```
coll.createIndex(new BasicDBObject("userid",1));
```

> If you have been using the MongoDB Java driver in its earlier version, you might have used the `ensureIndex` method to create an index if that is not available. This method is now deprecated and you have to use `createIndex` as shown.

Now, let's execute the `explain` plan query again and examine the result (we will show you just the relevant part of the statistics):

```
> db.indextest.find({userid: 5000}).explain("executionStats")
{
. . . .
  "executionStats":{
    "executionSuccess":true,
    "nReturned":0,
    "executionTimeMillis":0,
    "totalKeysExamined":1,
    "totalDocsExamined":1,
    "executionStages":{
      "stage":"FETCH",
      "nReturned":0,
      "executionTimeMillisEstimate":0,
      "works":1,
```

```
"advanced":0,
"needTime":0,
"needFetch":0,
"saveState":0,
"restoreState":0,
 "isEOF":1,
 "invalidates":0,
 "docsExamined":0,
 "alreadyHasObj":0,
 "inputStage":{
   "stage":"IXSCAN",
   "nReturned":0,
   "executionTimeMillisEstimate":0,
   "works":1,
   "advanced":0,
   "needTime":0,
   "needFetch":0,
   "saveState":0,
   "restoreState":0,
   "isEOF":1,
   "invalidates":0,
   "keyPattern":{
     "userid":1
   },
   "indexName":"userid_1",
   "isMultiKey":false,
   "direction":"forward",
   "indexBounds":{
     "userid":[
       "[\"1111\", \"1111\"]"
     ]
   },
   "keysExamined":0,
   "dupsTested":0,
   "dupsDropped":0,
```

```
        "seenInvalidated":0,

        "matchTested":0
    }
  },
    "allPlansExecution":[


    ]
  },
. . .
```

The `explain()` output is now a bit more complex; let's focus on the fields we are interested in. The number of `totalDocsExamined` documents is just one and the query is now instantaneous as the index named `userid_1` has been used. However, everything has its flip side. In this case, we will have super-fast queries at the price of slower inserts/updates as indexes have to be rewritten too. More storage has to be planned also since indexes will need it. However, that is now a peculiarity of MongoDB, but it is a clear assumption that is true on every database.

For the sake of completeness, we will mention that the `explain` function is also available on the Java side, by calling the `explain` method directly on a search string:

```java
BasicDBObject doc = new BasicDBObject("userid", "1111");
DBObject explainObject = coll.find(doc).explain();

System.out.println(explainObject) ;
```

Using compound indexes

The preceding examples are making the assumption that our indexed field is a prefix in the query. For example, consider the following search:

```java
BasicDBObject doc = new BasicDBObject("code", "1111").
append("userid",5000);

DBObject explainObject = coll.find(doc);
```

In this case, having defined the index on the `userid` field, this is not helping our query too much, as the index will come into play only after scanning the first key, that is, code. A solution, in this case, could be to create a compound index that is a handy solution if your search contains multiple criteria.

The following sample diagram illustrates a compound index using two fields, such as userid and code:

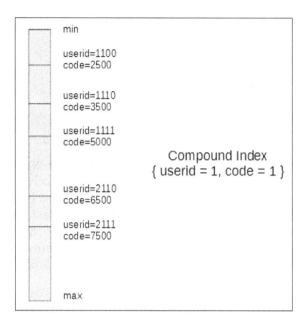

As you can see from the preceding figure, in a **Compound Index**, a single index structure holds references to multiple fields (**userid** and **code**) within a collection's documents.

Creating a **Compound Index** is not very different from creating a single index field. Using the fluent API provided by the BasicDBObject, you can append the keys and then create the index with that object:

```
DBObject obj = new BasicDBObject();
obj.put("userid", 1);
obj.put("code", 1);
coll.createIndex(obj);
```

You can run the **Compound Index** creation and verify that the search cursor is using the **Compound Index** and scanning only one document:

```
> db.indextest.find({userid: 5000, code:5000}).explain("executionStats")


{
. . . .

"executionStats":{
```

```
"executionSuccess":true,
"nReturned":0,
"executionTimeMillis":0,
"totalKeysExamined":1,
"totalDocsExamined":1,
"executionStages":{
  "stage":"FETCH",
  "nReturned":0,
  "executionTimeMillisEstimate":0,
  "works":1,
  "advanced":0,
  "needTime":0,
  "needFetch":0,
  "saveState":0,
  "restoreState":0,
  "isEOF":1,
  "invalidates":0,
  "docsExamined":0,
  "alreadyHasObj":0,
  "inputStage":{
    "stage":"IXSCAN",
    "nReturned":0,
    "executionTimeMillisEstimate":0,
    "works":1,
    "advanced":0,
    "needTime":0,
    "needFetch":0,
    "saveState":0,
    "restoreState":0,
    "isEOF":1,
    "invalidates":0,
    "keyPattern":{
      "userid":1,
        "code":1
```

```
      },
      "indexName":"userid_1_code_1",
      "isMultiKey":false,
      "direction":"forward",
      "indexBounds":{
        "userid":[
        "[\"1111\", \"1111\"]"
        ],
        "code":[
          "[MinKey, MaxKey]"
        ]
        },
        "keysExamined":0,
        "dupsTested":0,
        "dupsDropped":0,
        "seenInvalidated":0,
        "matchTested":0
      }
   },
     "allPlansExecution":[

   ]
  },
}
```

Using text indexes in your documents

MongoDB has support for text indexes that can be used to search strings of text contained in documents of a collection.

 Since version 2.6 of MongoDB, the text search feature is enabled by default, so you don't need to do anything in order to activate it.

In order to perform queries using the text index, you need to use the $text query operator. In the following example, we are creating a text index on the content key:

```
MongoClient mongoClient = new MongoClient("localhost", 27017);

DB db = mongoClient.getDB("sampledb");
```

```
DBCollection coll = db.getCollection("textitems");

coll.createIndex(new BasicDBObject("content", "text"));

coll.insert(new BasicDBObject().append("content", "mytext other
content"));

DBObject search = new BasicDBObject("$search", "mytext");

DBObject textSearch = new BasicDBObject("$text", search);

int count = coll.find(textSearch).count();
System.out.println("Found text search matches: " + count);
```

Once the index has been created, we will use the $text operator to perform a text
search on the collection, using the string of words contained in the $search operator:

```
MongoClient mongoClient = new MongoClient("localhost", 27017);

DB db = mongoClient.getDB("sampledb");

DBCollection coll = db.getCollection("textitems");

coll.insert(new BasicDBObject("_id", 1).append("text", "mytext"));

List<DBObject> list = coll.getIndexInfo();

for (DBObject obj:list)
  System.out.println(obj);
}
```

The method getIndexInfo returns a list of the indexes for this collection
as DBObject. This information is printed on the console, which in our case,
outputs the following:

```
{ "v" : 1 , "key" : { "_id" : 1} , "name" : "_id_" , "ns" :
"sampledb.textitems"}
```

Searching for text by language

Text search can be done using additional options such as language search, which
enables restricting the text search to a particular language. The list of languages
supported in this text search is contained in the driver documentation at
http://docs.mongodb.org/manual/reference/text-search-languages/.

Here is a full example that shows how to restrict your searches only to English words by means of the `$language` operator:

```
MongoClient mongoClient = new MongoClient("localhost", 27017);

DB db = mongoClient.getDB("sampledb");

DBCollection coll = db.getCollection("textitems");

coll.createIndex(new BasicDBObject("textcontent", "text"));

coll.insert(new BasicDBObject("_id", 0).append("textcontent",
    "Some data"));
coll.insert(new BasicDBObject("_id", 1).append("textcontent",
    "Other data"));
coll.insert(new BasicDBObject("_id", 2).append("textcontent", "Not
    important"));

BasicDBObject search = new BasicDBObject("$search", "data");

DBObject textSearch = new BasicDBObject("$text",
    search.append("$language", "english"));

int matchCount = coll.find(textSearch).count();
System.out.println("Found lanuguagage matches: " + matchCount);
```

The expected output, from the last line of code, is to print:

```
Found language matches: 2
```

Searching for text by score

A common requirement for a text search engine is to provide a score, for example, in the case of searches including a complex set of words. Score search can be done by setting the `textScore` parameter in the `$meta` projection operator.

 The score represents the relevance of a document to a given text search query.

The following example shows how to return the score in a search by means of the metadata associated with the query:

```
DBObject scoreSearch = new BasicDBObject("score", new
DBObject("$meta", "textScore"));
```

```
DBObject doc = coll.findOne(textSearch, scoreSearch);

System.out.println("Highest scoring document: "+ doc);
```

Coding bulk operations

One of the highlights available since MongoDB 2.6 is the new bulk write operations. Bulk operations allow building a list of write operations to be executed in bulk for a single collection. The Java driver for MongoDB includes a new bulk API as well, which allows your applications to leverage these new operations using a fluent-style API.

First of all, let's explore this API that can be executed using two main styles:

- **Ordered bulk operations**: Every operation will be executed in the order they are added to the bulk operation, halting when there's an error
- **Unordered bulk operations**: These operations are executed in parallel and neither guarantee order of execution, nor do they stop when an error occurs

First, let's see an example of OrderedBulkOperation:

```
BulkWriteOperation builder =
    collection.initializeOrderedBulkOperation();

builder.insert(new BasicDBObject("item", "A1"));
builder.insert(new BasicDBObject("item", "A2"));
builder.insert(new BasicDBObject("item", "A3"));

builder.find(new BasicDBObject("item", "A1")).updateOne(new
    BasicDBObject("$set", new BasicDBObject("A1", "AX")));

BulkWriteResult result = builder.execute();

System.out.println("Bulk Completed: Inserted documents " +
    result.getInsertedCount());
System.out.println("Bulk Completed: Modified documents " +
    result.getModifiedCount());
```

As you can see, an instance of the BulkWriteOperation class is created using the initializeOrderedBulkOperation method of the collection class. Operations are added using the fluent API available in the BulkWriteOperation.

The expected output of the preceding execution will be as follows:

```
Bulk Completed: Inserted documents 3
Bulk Completed: Modified documents 1
```

Finally, the `BulkWriteResult` is used as a wrapper that contains the results of the `Bulk.execute()` method.

The same code written using an unordered bulk operation can be coded this way:

```
BulkWriteOperation builder =
  collection.initializeUnorderedBulkOperation();

builder.insert(new BasicDBObject("item", "A1"));
builder.insert(new BasicDBObject("item", "A2"));
builder.insert(new BasicDBObject("item", "A3"));

builder.find(new BasicDBObject("item", "A1")).updateOne(new
  BasicDBObject("$set", new BasicDBObject("A1", "AX")));

BulkWriteResult result = builder.execute();
```

Comparing plain inserts with BulkWriteOperations

Bulk operations are most useful when you have a batch of inserts/updates which need to be executed in one single shot. The advantage in terms of performance is notable. As a proof of evidence, we will compare the execution of a batch of 10,000 documents using the default approach:

```
long l1 = System.currentTimeMillis();

for (int ii=0;ii<10000;ii++) {
  DBObject doc = new BasicDBObject("name","frank")
    .append("age", 31)
    .append("info", new BasicDBObject("email",
    "frank@mail.com").append("phone", "222-111-444"));

  coll.insert(doc);
}

long l2 = System.currentTimeMillis();

System.out.println(l2-l1);
```

By running the above example, 10,000 inserts are performed in 7421 ms. Let's reengineer the code to use bulk operations:

```
long l1 = System.currentTimeMillis();

BulkWriteOperation builder = coll.initializeOrderedBulkOperation();

for (int ii=0;ii<10000;ii++) {
    DBObject doc = new BasicDBObject("name","frank")
        .append("age", 31)
        .append("info", new BasicDBObject("email",
        "frank@mail.com").append("phone", "222-111-444"));

    builder.insert(doc);
}
BulkWriteResult result = builder.execute();

long l2 = System.currentTimeMillis();

System.out.println(l2-l1);
```

The second execution was completed in as little as 1535 ms.

You can further reduce the execution by switching to an unordered bulk execution:

```
BulkWriteOperation builder =
    coll.initializeUnorderedBulkOperation();
```

This will bring down the time to even less, that is, 1446 ms to insert 10,000 records.

Summary

In this chapter, we have gone through some advanced features available in the MongoDB Java driver, and we examined some strategies for mapping Java objects to MongoDB documents. The solutions we have covered will fit into many practical scenarios. We now need to change the perspective of our examples a bit as we move into an enterprise context. In the next chapter, we will show you how to use the knowledge we have built so far to create a Java Enterprise application using MongoDB as the storage.

4
MongoDB in the Java EE 7 Enterprise Environment

In this chapter, we will dive into the **Java Enterprise Edition** (**JEE**) API by creating a simple web application, which uses MongoDB as storage. We will demonstrate how this technology can leverage a real-world scenario using simple and lean constructs. Some kind of exposure with Java EE technology will help you to get quickly to the point; however, a brief overview of the Java EE platform will be provided. In more detail, here is what we will discuss in this chapter:

- A brief introduction to the Java EE platform
- Design and development of the application and tools required to construct them
- Deploying the application to a Java EE certified application server

Entering into the Java EE land

Writing an application for the IT industry can be a big challenge for any developer, as it needs to address some important concerns such as security, portability, and high availability just to mention a few. Most of them need to also interact with other systems and be managed from a central point. Using the JEE platform, you can leverage all these features and more, focusing on the most important concern, that is your business requirements.

The Java EE platform development is handled through the **Java Community Process (JCP)**, which is a community in charge of developing specifications for all Java technologies. This community is composed of top IT industry experts that have set the **Java Specification Requests (JSRs)** to delineate the Java EE technologies. Thanks to the work of the Java Community, developing applications with Java EE is now easier and more powerful at every new release. The set of available APIs has grown too, making up a big picture of technology, which is shown in the following diagram:

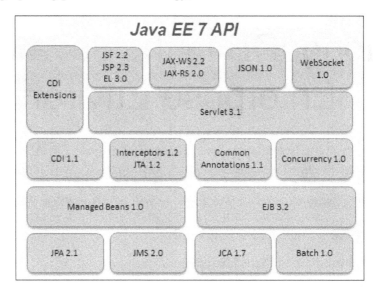

We have to admit that a large amount of available APIs might be overwhelming for a beginner who is looking for a quick head start with this technology. Fortunately, you don't need to be scared by that picture as it's absolutely not needed to learn all of that, but you can code real-world applications with as little as a couple of the above building blocks. In our case, we will pick up some core components such as:

- A technology for developing the end user interface such as **Java Server Faces (JSF)**
- An API that can bridge your requests to your MongoDB applications such as RESTFul web services
- Some glue between the frontend and the backend and the ability to let the Java EE container to manage objects such as MongoDB client connections. We will use **Context and Dependency Injection (CDI)** for this purpose.

In order to use the preceding features, we need a JEE Container at first, which is a special kind of Java application that is compliant with JEE specifications and can be, therefore, used to execute your JEE applications. Let's pick up a JEE Container at first, then we will suggest some tooling that can be used to simplify the development of JEE applications.

Getting a Java EE Container

Running Java EE applications can be done by means of open source solutions and vendor products as well. The choice between open source and vendor solutions is out of the scope of this book as it is often not a matter of technology features, but it is well shaped also by the commercial choices of your IT company. We will use an open source product called WildFly, formerly known as the JBoss application server, which is now developed by Red Hat (http://www.redhat.com).

 As an author of some books about WildFly, I hope you don't find me biased on this choice. Besides, you can be assured that you will be using an advanced, stable, and well-known in the trenches middleware product.

Downloading WildFly

You can freely download WildFly from http://www.wildfly.org.

Select the latest stable release which is, at the time of writing, 8.2. WildFly ships as a ZIP file so all you have to do is a postinstallation job, unzipping it in a folder of your machine:

```
unzip wildfly-8.2.0.Final.zip
```

In order to start WildFly, it is recommended to set the JAVA_HOME variable so that it points to the location where you have installed Java. You can add this information to your system as follows:

- **Linux users**: Enter the following script in your .profile/.bash_profile script (substitute this with the actual location of Java)

  ```
  export JAVA_HOME=/usr/java/jdk1.7.0_71
  ```

- **Windows users**: Right-click on the My Computer icon on your desktop and select **Properties**. Then select **Advanced Tab** contained in the **Environment Variables** button. Under **System Variable**, click on **New**. Enter the variable name as JAVA_HOME and value the Java install path. Click on **OK** and then on **Apply Changes**.

Starting WildFly and testing the installation

WildFly start up scripts are located in the `bin` folder of the root installation. You can basically start it in two different modes:

- Standalone mode, which means that the application server will be a single Java process, where applications can be executed

- Domain mode, in case you want to manage a set of application servers from a central Java process called the Domain controller

Discussing the domain mode is out of the scope of this book; therefore, we will use the single process mode (standalone). No changes to your code will be required to run the application in domain mode.

Hence, you can start the application server by executing the following command from the `bin` folder:

`/standalone.sh`

Windows users should use the equivalent batch script:

`standalone.bat`

In the server console, you should find something like this, at the end of startup process:

```
10:07:16,137 INFO  [org.jboss.as] (Controller Boot Thread) JBAS015961:
Http management interface listening on http://127.0.0.1:9990/management

10:07:16,140 INFO  [org.jboss.as] (Controller Boot Thread) JBAS015951:
Admin console listening on http://127.0.0.1:9990

10:07:16,141 INFO  [org.jboss.as] (Controller Boot Thread) JBAS015874:
WildFly 8.2.0.Final "Tweek" started in 29033ms - Started 255 of 310
services (92 services are lazy, passive or on-demand)
```

You can verify that the server is reachable from the network by simply pointing your browser to the application server's welcome page, which is reachable, by default, at the address `http://localhost:8080`.

Designing our application

Our application will be a simple bookstore which contains a list of book titles. A start up class will be in charge of adding books to the bookstore. Once executed, the user will be able to purchase books and perform searches over the titles.

Business use cases such as payment checks are excluded from this basic example as this is not a typical database concern; hence, it is out of the scope of this book. Nevertheless, you can easily include this functionality by adding any Stateful component (such as Stateful beans or Session Scoped beans).

On the other hand, a database concern is updating the available list of books, once the user purchases a copy of it.

Every application starts from a proper data schema design, so our first step will be to define the database structure and then to create the Java EE interfaces, starting with those directly involved with data CRUD, and then moving on to the customer view design.

Designing the schema

Our MongoDB documents will be created in the following storage:

- Database: `javaee7`
- Collection: `bookstore`

The following is the list of keys we will store in our MongoDB document:

- Book ID (automatically generated)
- Book title (String)
- Book author (String)
- Book type (String)
- Book price (Double)
- Book copies (Integer)

Here is an example document that we will use in our application:

```
{
        "_id" : ObjectId("5541ea47438724845af4cff7"),
        "title" : "The Hobbit",
        "author" : "J.R.R. Tolkien",
        "type" : "Fantasy",
        "price" : 8,
        "copies" : 10
}
```

All database objects will be created by our Java Enterprise application, so right now your only concern will be to start up MongoDB.

Building up the Enterprise project with NetBeans

Our Java Enterprise application will now be created, step by step.

We will use NetBeans for coding and building our project. Our helping hand will be Maven, which is a de facto standard used by Java developers to arrange for a standard application structure, compile, deploy, and test it. Being an extensible framework based on plugins, the capabilities of Maven can be even expanded far beyond the points mentioned earlier.

First of all, however, we need to configure it so that it can be used in combination with the WildFly application server; the upcoming section details it.

Configuring WildFly on NetBeans

Since release 8.0.2 of NetBeans, you can directly add the WildFly server to the list of available servers, without the need to download it as a separate plugin. Start NetBeans at first. From the left side of its GUI, select the **Services** tab and right-click on **Servers**, as shown in the following screenshot:

Select **Add Server**. The server wizard will start. As the first option, select **WildFly Application Server** from the list of available application servers. Click on the **Next** button to move ahead to the next step:

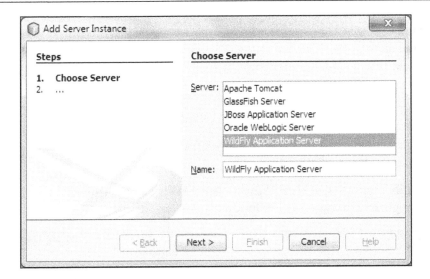

In the following window, select the location where WildFly is installed and pick up the server configuration file to be used (`standalone.xml` is the default configuration file):

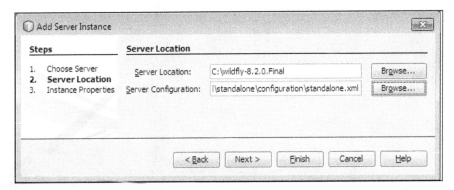

Click on **Finish**. As you can see from the following screenshot, now the **WildFly Application Server** is enlisted among the available services by expanding the **Servers** option:

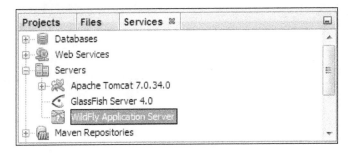

Creating our project

In order to create our project, we will use a Maven project. Maven is a popular software and release management tool which buys you:

- A standard structure for all your Java projects
- A centralized and automatic management of dependencies

Most development environments are Maven friendly; this means, you don't need to download any additional plugins.

From the **File** menu, select **New Project**. Select **Web Application** as displayed in the **Maven** categories, as shown in the following screenshot:

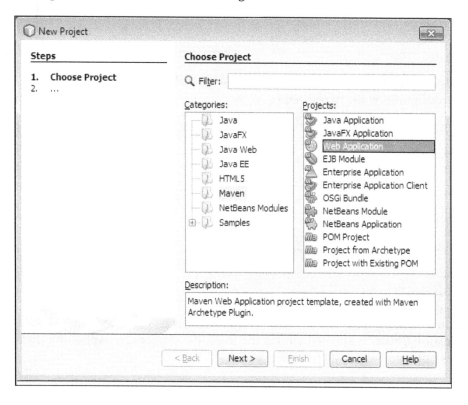

Click on **Next**. The following window will be displayed:

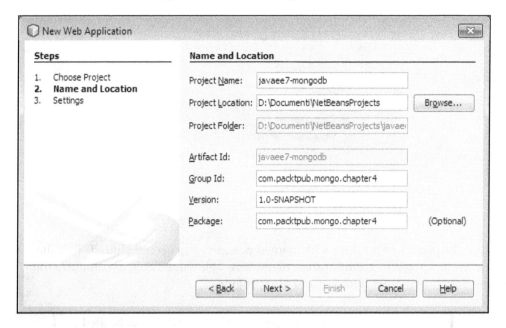

Enter the **Project Name**, its location on your filesystem, the **Group Id**, **Version**, and **Package** information. Then click on **Next**.

 The **Group Id** in Maven terms is a naming schema used by your Maven project. It generally matches with the root package of your application.

In the following window, select **WildFly Application Server** as **Server** and **Java EE 7 Web** as **Java EE Version**:

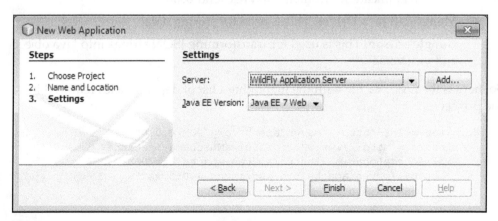

Click on **Finish** to create the Maven project. The following screenshot shows the basic structure of your project view:

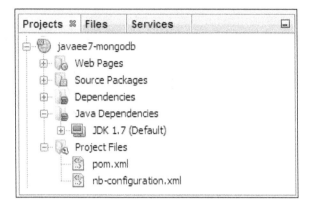

Within the project files folder a file named pom.xml has been included. This file is the Maven project's configuration file, where you will be able to configure the dependencies on other libraries and also plugins.

 Maven plugins are just Java libraries, which can be used to empower your Maven with additional capabilities such as compiling, deploying, and testing your code.

In order to compile your project, you will need to specify the dependencies, that is, the library which needs to be used by our project. We will start with the following set of libraries in our project:

- **Enterprise Java Beans**: This is used to code a start up class in our project
- **Java Server Faces and Context Dependency Injection**: This is used to code the web application's frontend and backend beans
- **Mongo DB Java Driver**: This is used for storing data
- **Google's Gson**: This is used for transforming JSON strings into Java objects and vice versa

So, here is the pom.xml file with the highlighted list of dependencies required in the project:

```xml
<project xmlns="http://maven.apache.org/POM/4.0.0"
    xmlns:xsi="http://www.w3.org/2001/XMLSchema-instance"
     xsi:schemaLocation="http://maven.apache.org/POM/4.0.0
        http://maven.apache.org/xsd/maven-4.0.0.xsd">
    <modelVersion>4.0.0</modelVersion>
```

```xml
<groupId>com.packtpub.mongo.chapter4</groupId>
<artifactId>javaee7-mongodb</artifactId>
<version>1.0-SNAPSHOT</version>
<packaging>war</packaging>
<name>javaee7-mongodb</name>
<properties>
    <endorsed.dir>${project.build.directory}/endorsed</endorsed.dir>
<project.build.sourceEncoding>UTF-8
</project.build.sourceEncoding>
</properties>

<dependencyManagement>
  <dependencies>
    <dependency>
      <groupId>org.wildfly.bom</groupId>
      <artifactId>jboss-javaee-7.0-with-all</artifactId>
      <version>8.2.0.Final</version>
      <type>pom</type>
      <scope>import</scope>
    </dependency>
  </dependencies>
</dependencyManagement>

<dependencies>
  <dependency>
    <groupId>org.mongodb</groupId>
    <artifactId>mongo-java-driver</artifactId>
    <version>2.12.4</version>
  </dependency>

  <dependency>
    <groupId>javax.enterprise</groupId>
    <artifactId>cdi-api</artifactId>
    <scope>provided</scope>
  </dependency>

  <dependency>
    <groupId>org.jboss.spec.javax.faces</groupId>
    <artifactId>jboss-jsf-api_2.2_spec</artifactId>
    <scope>provided</scope>
  </dependency>

  <dependency>
```

```xml
      <groupId>org.jboss.spec.javax.ejb</groupId>
      <artifactId>jboss-ejb-api_3.2_spec</artifactId>
      <scope>provided</scope>
    </dependency>

    <dependency>
      <groupId>org.jboss.spec.javax.annotation</groupId>
      <artifactId>jboss-annotations-api_1.2_spec</artifactId>
      <scope>provided</scope>
    </dependency>

    <dependency>
      <groupId>com.google.code.gson</groupId>
      <artifactId>gson</artifactId>
      <version>2.3.1</version>
    </dependency>

    <dependency>
      <groupId>org.jboss.resteasy</groupId>
      <artifactId>jaxrs-api</artifactId>
    </dependency>
  </dependencies>

  <build>
    <finalName>${project.artifactId}</finalName>
    <plugins>
      <plugin>
        <groupId>org.apache.maven.plugins</groupId>
        <artifactId>maven-compiler-plugin</artifactId>
        <version>3.1</version>
        <configuration>
          <source>1.7</source>
          <target>1.7</target>
          <compilerArguments>
            <endorseddirs>${endorsed.dir}</endorseddirs>
          </compilerArguments>
        </configuration>
      </plugin>
      <plugin>
        <groupId>org.apache.maven.plugins</groupId>
        <artifactId>maven-war-plugin</artifactId>
        <version>2.3</version>
        <configuration>
          <failOnMissingWebXml>false</failOnMissingWebXml>
```

```
        </configuration>
      </plugin>
    </plugins>
  </build>
</project>
```

 You can see that we have also included a **Bill of Materials (BOM)** at the top of our dependencies. This is a handy option so that you don't need to specify each of WildFly's library versions, as they are maintained in the external BOM file.

We are done with the project's skeleton. Allow a couple of minutes to NetBeans to load all the required dependencies, and then you can go for the real classes, which will make up your application.

Adding Java classes

The first Java class we will add is named `Book` and will be used to map MongoDB documents. It contains the same field as the corresponding keys of the document:

```java
package com.packtpub.mongo.chapter4.bean;

public class Book {

    String title;
    String author;
    String type;
    double price;
    int copies;

    public Book() { }

    public Book(String title, String author, String type, double price)
    {
        super();
        this.title = title;
        this.author = author;
        this.type = type;
        this.price = price;
        this.copies = 10;
    }

    // Getter and Setters omitted for brevity
}
```

Now that we have the basic structure to host Mongo documents, we need to handle the connection toward MongoDB. Within the Java Enterprise environment, there is a better alternative than the following piece of your code around your classes:

```
MongoClient mongoClient = new MongoClient("localhost", 27017);
```

Instead of the preceding code, we will create a CDI producer, which will be in charge of creating an instance of the `MongoClient` object and share it with the classes of your application. So, add a class named `Producer` to your project:

```
package com.packtpub.mongo.chapter4.producer;

import com.mongodb.MongoClient;
import com.packtpub.mongo.chapter4.ejb.SchemaSetup;
import java.util.logging.Level;
import java.util.logging.Logger;
import javax.enterprise.context.ApplicationScoped;
@ApplicationScoped

public class Producer {
private static final Logger LOGGER =
    Logger.getLogger(Producer.class.getName());

    @Produces
    public MongoClient mongoClient() {
      try {
        return new MongoClient("localhost", 27017);
      } catch (UnknownHostException e) {
        LOGGER.log(Level.SEVERE, e.getMessage(), e);
      }
      return null;
    }
}
```

> `Producers` are a useful addition provided by CDI, which can be used when the concrete type of the objects to be injected may vary at runtime or when the objects require some custom initialization that is not performed by the bean constructor.

Now, we will add the `Controller` class named `BookStore`, which receives input from the user interface and constructs the list of available books:

```
package com.packtpub.mongo.chapter4.controller;

import com.google.gson.Gson;
```

```java
import com.mongodb.BasicDBObject;
import com.mongodb.DB;
import com.mongodb.DBCollection;
import com.mongodb.DBCursor;
import com.mongodb.DBObject;
import com.mongodb.MongoClient;
import com.mongodb.util.JSON;

import java.io.Serializable;
import java.util.ArrayList;
import java.util.List;
import javax.annotation.PostConstruct;
import javax.enterprise.inject.Model;
import javax.inject.Inject;
import com.packtpub.mongo.chapter4.bean.Book;

@Model
public class BookStore {

  @Inject
  MongoClient mongoClient;

  List<Book> listBooks;

  String filter;

  @PostConstruct
  private void init() {
    doQuery();
  }

  public void doQuery() {
    listBooks = query();
  }
  public List<Book> query() {
    Gson gson = new Gson();
    DB db = mongoClient.getDB("javaee7");
    DBCollection coll = db.getCollection("bookstore");
    DBCursor cursor = null;
    if (filter == null || filter.trim().length() == 0) {
      cursor = coll.find();
    }
    else {
```

```
      DBObject q = new BasicDBObject();
      q.put("title",  java.util.regex.Pattern.compile(filter));
      cursor = coll.find(q);
    }

  List<Book> list = new ArrayList<>();
  try {
    while (cursor.hasNext()) {
      DBObject obj = cursor.next();

      list.add(gson.fromJson(obj.toString(), Book.class));

    }
  } finally {
    cursor.close();
  }
  return list;
}

public void buy(Book book) {
  System.out.println("Buy book!!!!!"+book);
  Gson gson = new Gson();

  int copiesLeft = book.getCopies() - 1;
  DB db = mongoClient.getDB("javaee7");

  DBCollection coll = db.getCollection("bookstore");

  DBObject newDocument = new BasicDBObject();
  newDocument.append("$set",
    new BasicDBObject().append("copies", copiesLeft));

  DBObject searchQuery = (DBObject)
    JSON.parse(gson.toJson(book));
  coll.update(searchQuery, newDocument);

  listBooks = query();

  }

}
```

And now, let's discuss the most relevant parts of this class. First of all, there is a @Model annotation at the top of it. This is a CDI stereotype that can be used on CDI beans in order to achieve two things:

- Defining a request scope for the class. It means that the class will be created and destroyed according to the user's request life cycle.
- Guaranteeing expression language visibility. It means that the class can be used in our UI.

Next, we are using the @Inject annotation to let the container provide an instance of the MongoClient class, which is actually done by the Producer class we just coded.

The query and buy methods are our business methods, which are used for listing the books and for purchasing them respectively. If you have gone through the Gson API discussed in the previous chapter, this code should be quite intuitive for you.

Within the query method, you will find a search expression, which is used to filter among the titles using a regular expression pattern. The purpose of the following block of code is to provide a SQL LIKE functionality during the search:

```
BasicDBObject q = new BasicDBObject();
q.put("title", java.util.regex.Pattern.compile(filter));
cursor = coll.find(q);
```

The list of available books is ultimately maintained into the List<Book> listBooks collection, which is updated every time a book is purchased.

The preceding two classes are sufficient to make up the backbone of a Java EE application. We will include one more class to provide some available books when the application is deployed:

```
package com.packtpub.mongo.chapter4.ejb;

import com.google.gson.Gson;
import com.mongodb.DB;
import com.mongodb.DBCollection;
import com.mongodb.DBObject;
import com.mongodb.MongoClient;
import com.mongodb.util.JSON;
import com.packtpub.mongo.chapter4.bean.Book;
import java.util.logging.Level;
import java.util.logging.Logger;
import javax.annotation.PostConstruct;
import javax.ejb.Startup;
import javax.ejb.Singleton;
import javax.inject.Inject;
```

```java
@Singleton
@Startup

public class SchemaSetup {

private static final Logger LOGGER = Logger.getLogger(SchemaSetup.
class.getName());

  @Inject
  MongoClient mongoClient;

  @PostConstruct
  public void createSchema() {
    try {

        DB db = mongoClient.getDB("javaee7");

        DBCollection coll = db.getCollection("bookstore");
        coll.drop();
        coll = db.getCollection("bookstore");

        Book[] book = new Book[5];
        book[0] = new Book("A Tale Of Two Cities", "Charles
Dickens","Novel", 10);
        book[1] = new Book("Le Petit Prince", "Antoine de Saint-
Exupery","Novel", 8);
        book[2] = new Book("The Da Vinci Code", "Dan Brown", "thriller",
12);
        book[3] = new Book("Think and Grow Rich", "Napoleon
Hill","Motivational", 10);
        book[4] = new Book("The Hobbit", "J.R.R. Tolkien", "Fantasy",
8);
        Gson gson = new Gson();

        for (Book b : book) {
          DBObject obj = (DBObject) JSON.parse(gson.toJson(b));
          coll.insert(obj);
        }

    } catch (Exception e) {
      LOGGER.log(Level.SEVERE, e.getMessage(), e);
    }
  }
}
```

The preceding class is a singleton EJB, which means only one instance of this class will be created by the container. Thanks to the @Startup annotation, the createSchema method, which is annotated with @PostConstruct, will be executed when the application is deployed.

Inside the createSchema method, we first clean up our existing collection of books, and then, we create a new collection by using a combination of the MongoDB driver and Google Gson API.

The server side part is completed. We need one view for displaying the book titles and a couple of buttons to perform a filter on the titles and to purchase a book respectively. The following is the index.xhtml page, which needs to be added to the project's web pages:

```html
<html xmlns="http://www.w3.org/1999/xhtml"
  xmlns:h="http://java.sun.com/jsf/html"
  xmlns:f="http://java.sun.com/jsf/core"
  xmlns:c="http://java.sun.com/jsp/jstl/core">
 <h:head></h:head>

<h:body>

  <h:form id="bookstore">
    <h:panelGrid >
      <h:outputLabel value="Filter title: " style="font-weight:bold"
/>
      <h:inputText value="#{bookStore.filter}" />
      <h:commandButton actionListener="#{bookStore.doQuery}"
styleClass="buttons" value="Search" />
      <h:dataTable value="#{bookStore.listBooks}" var="item"
styleClass="table"
        headerClass="table header"
        rowClasses="table-odd-row,table-even-row">
        <h:column>
          <f:facet name="header">Title</f:facet>
          <h:outputText value="#{item.title}" />
        </h:column>
        <h:column>
          <f:facet name="header">Author</f:facet>
          <h:outputText value="#{item.author}" />
        </h:column>

        <h:column>
          <f:facet name="header">Price</f:facet>
```

```
                <h:outputText value="#{item.price}" />
            </h:column>
            <h:column>
              <f:facet name="header">Type</f:facet>
              <h:outputText value="#{item.type}" />
            </h:column>
            <h:column>
              <f:facet name="header">Copies</f:facet>
              <h:outputText value="#{item.copies}"/>
            </h:column>

            <h:column>
              <f:facet name="header">Buy</f:facet>
               <h:commandButton actionListener="#{bookStore.buy(item)}"
    rendered="#{item.copies > 0}"
                 styleClass="buttons" value="Buy" />
            </h:column>
          </h:dataTable>
        </h:panelGrid>

      </h:form>


   </h:body>
   </html>
```

The preceding code contains a few basic JSF components such as inputText, which is a HTML text field used to perform a filter over the title field. The next component is dataTable, which is used to display tabular data contained in the listBooks list in BookStore. Within dataTable, every field is referenced through the variable item, so that we have a tabular view of all our BookStore.

Finally, a Buy button is included, which submits the execution to the buy method of the BookStore bean, passing as an argument the item on which the button was clicked.

 Just to remind you, the BookStore beans can be referenced from the user interface as we have tagged it with the @Model annotation. As no specific name has been chosen for this bean, it will be referenced using its default EL name, which is BookStore.

Compiling and deploying the project

Compiling and deploying the project is just one click away from you, provided that you have added a WildFly application server to your list of services. Simply right-click on your project and choose **Run**. A sequence of operations will be triggered:

1. At first, the WildFly application server will start.
2. The web application will be deployed.
3. The `index.xhtml` page will be displayed.

If you are not using NetBeans, simply follow the next section, which will detail a generic compilation and deployment procedure, which can be used from the shell prompt or wrapped by your development environment.

Compiling and deploying from the shell

Any Maven project can be compiled and packaged by executing the following goals:

`mvn clean install`

This will generate an artifact named `javaee7-mongodb.war` file, which needs to be deployed on the application server. The simplest way to do it is to copy the file into `standalone/deployments` of WildFly.

If you want to automate the distribution of the web application, we would suggest adding Maven's WildFly plugin, which will handle the deployment for you. In order to do that, you need to add the following plugin definition at the bottom of your `pom.xml` file:

```xml
<build>
  <finalName>${project.artifactId}</finalName>
  <plugins>
    <plugin>
      <groupId>org.wildfly.plugins</groupId>
      <artifactId>wildfly-maven-plugin</artifactId>
      <version>1.0.2.Final</version>
    </plugin>
  </plugins>
</build>
```

Now, with the plugin in place, you can perform compilation, packaging, and deployment with a single command:

`mvn clean install wildfly:deploy`

A successful execution will terminate with an output like the following one:

```
INFO: JBoss Remoting version 4.0.3.Final
[INFO] ---------------------------------------------------------------
------
[INFO] BUILD SUCCESS
[INFO] ---------------------------------------------------------------
------
[INFO] Total time: 12.269 s
[INFO] Finished at: 2015-04-30T10:39:35+01:00
[INFO] Final Memory: 14M/37M
[INFO] ---------------------------------------------------------------
------
```

Running the application

Whatever is your development environment, you will end up with the web application deployed on WildFly. So, now, browse over the following URL in order to test the application:

```
http://localhost:8080/javaee7-mongodb/index.xhtml
```

Here is how your application should look like (We have omitted to include the stylesheets used in the index.xhtml page for the sake of brevity. You can find the complete source code of the book in the download area.):

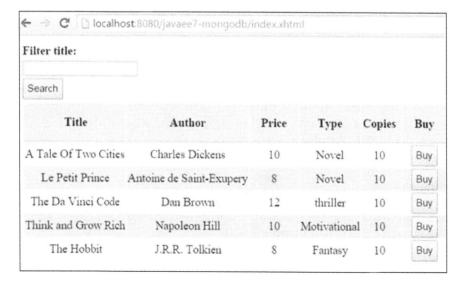

You can try to see how the application works by clicking on the **Buy** button, which will decrease the count of the available book copies. Entering some text into the **Filter title** field and clicking on **Search** will restrict the search only to titles containing that text:

Exposing the application to external clients

One of the biggest advantages of using JSON to represent your application's data is that you can easily integrate with other systems that support JSON and display its data natively. In order to be able to expose our data to external systems, we need to, however, wrap our CDI beans with some compatible exchange format such as **REST Services**. This will put the MongoDB data at your fingertips with just a couple of additions to our project!

A RESTful web service exposes a set of resources to external clients. Resources are identified by URIs, which provide a simple and uniform way to manipulate server-side resources using standard HTTP commands such as GET, POST, PUT, and DELETE.

Adding RESTful web services to our application

First of all, we will include the org.jboss.resteasy dependency, which is the actual implementation of REST services in WildFly:

```
<dependency>
  <groupId>org.jboss.resteasy</groupId>
  <artifactId>jaxrs-api</artifactId>
</dependency>
```

Getting to grips with REST web services is not a complicated matter. We need to specify the URI pattern, which will be used to access our services, the type of resources, which are produced (or consumed) by our services and, of course, the implementation.

Let's add a new Java class named `BookService` to our project with the following implementation:

```java
package com.packtpub.mongo.chapter4.ws;
import com.packtpub.mongo.chapter4.bean.Book;
import com.packtpub.mongo.chapter4.controller.BookStore;
import java.util.List;
import javax.inject.Inject;

import javax.ws.rs.*;
import javax.ws.rs.core.MediaType;
import javax.ws.rs.core.Response;

@Path("/bookstore")
public class BookService {

  @Inject
  BookStore bookstore;

  @GET
  @Produces(MediaType.APPLICATION_JSON)
  public List<Book> query() {

    return bookstore.getListBooks();
  }

  @POST
  @Consumes(MediaType.APPLICATION_JSON)
  public Response buyBook(Book b) {

    Book book = bookstore.checkAvailability(b);

    if (book == null) {
      return Response.ok("Book not found sorry!").build();
    }

    if (book.getCopies() > 0) {
      bookstore.buy(book);
      return Response.ok("Book purchased!").build();
    }
```

```
else {
  return Response.ok("No more copies available
    sorry!").build();
}


   }
}
```

Even if this is your first green bar with REST services, the preceding code should not look too complicated. At first, we have stated that our REST service will be available through the /bookstore URI path. Then, as this class is just a wrapper to our BookStore class, we have injected one instance of it inside our service.

We have then added two methods:

- The query method which is triggered by an HTTP GET and executes a query on the BookStore class, returning the list of books in the JSON format
- The buyBook method, which, on the other hand, is triggered by an HTTP POST checks for availability at first and then it executes the purchase.

In order to be able to use the buyBook method, we have to enrich our BookStore class with the method checkAvailability, which retrieves the actual book document by searching for the title and author as follows:

```
public class BookStore implements {
  . . . .
  public Book checkAvailability(Book book) {
    Gson gson = new Gson();

    DB db = mongoClient.getDB("javaee7");

    DBCollection coll = db.getCollection("bookstore");

    DBObject query = new BasicDBObject("title", book.getTitle());
    query.append("author", book.getAuthor());

    DBObject obj = coll.findOne(query);

    if (obj == null)
      return null;

    return gson.fromJson(obj.toString(), Book.class);


  }
}
```

Besides, in order to activate REST services on WildFly, we need to include a class that extends `javax.ws.rs.ApplicationPath` in our project, which also specifies the URI path to be used by REST services:

```
package com.packtpub.mongo.chapter4.ws;

@ApplicationPath("/rest")

public class RESTActivator extends Application {

}
```

Compiling and deploying the application

As usual, you can perform compilation, packaging, and deployment with a single click from NetBeans by selecting the project and right-clicking on **Run**. If you are not using NetBeans, just issue the following command from the shell:

```
mvn clean install wildfly:deploy
```

In order to test our application, we need to perform a request to the following URL:

```
http://localhost:8080/javaee7-mongodb/rest/bookstore
```

If the request is a GET request, the `query` method of the REST service will be triggered. On the other hand, if you are executing a POST request, the `buyBook` process will start.

There are plenty of solutions available to perform HTTP requests, for example, if you are on a Linux machine you can just use the `curl` command as follows to issue a GET request, which will return the list of books in the JSON format:

```
curl -H "Content-Type: application/json" -X GET
http://localhost:8080/javaee7-
mongodb/rest/bookstorehttp://localhost:8080/javaee7-
mongodb/rest/bookstore
```

The following content should be returned:

```
[{"title":"A Tale Of Two Cities","author":"Charles Dickens","type":"Nove
l","price":10,"copies":10},{"title":"Le Petit Prince","author":"Antoine
de Saint-Exupery","type":"Novel","price":8,"copies":10},{"title":"The Da
Vinci Code","author":"Dan Brown","type":"thriller","price":12,"copies":10
},{"title":"Think and Grow Rich","author":"Napoleon Hill","type":"Motivat
ional","price":10,"copies":10},{"title":"The Hobbit","author":"J.R.R. Tol
kien","type":"Fantasy","price":8,"copies":10}]
```

You can execute a POST request as well by passing the `title` and `author` parameters as follows:

```
curl -H "Content-Type: application/json" -X POST -d
'{"title":"titolo1","author":"author1"}'
http://localhost:8080/javaee7-mongodb/rest/bookstore
```

You should expect a `Book purchased` return string from the preceding command line.

Summary

In this chapter, we have learned how to create a Java Enterprise application just by adding a few classes to a web project. Thanks to the improvements in the Java EE specification, now coding an application requires very little code and minimal configuration. The project that we have created can be used as a template for your applications, which will use MongoDB as the foundation for storing data.

Some other solutions do exist, which can make the access to your MongoDB storage transparent so that you can adapt your code to other databases as well.

In the next chapter, we will discuss Hibernate **Object/Grid Mapper (OGM)**, which provides **Java Persistence API (JPA)** support for NoSQL solutions.

5
Managing Data Persistence with MongoDB and JPA

In this chapter, you will learn how to develop a Java Enterprise application using a standard API such as the Java Persistence API and an implementation of it. It is also called Hibernate **Object/Grid Mapper (OGM)**, which provides the **Java Persistence API (JPA)** support for NoSQL solutions such as MongoDB. The list of topics we will discuss are as follows:

- An introduction to the Java Persistence API
- Using Hibernate OGM to map MongoDB documents
- Developing and deploying a web application that uses Hibernate OGM as the persistence layer for your entities

An overview of the Java Persistence API

The earlier chapter was a gentle introduction to MongoDB in the **Java Enterprise Edition (JEE)** API. You learned how to engineer a simple web application using the MongoDB driver as a persistence layer. This can be a good solution for simple projects using just one data source. Often, it will be required to access multiple persistence layers in a neutral way, without coding the specific database query language. The standard API used for this purpose is the JPA, which can be implemented using different providers that are nothing but interfaces toward a data source.

The JPA has been inspired by **object-relational mapping (ORM)** frameworks, such as Hibernate, and uses annotations to map objects to a relational database. Each Java class mapping a database object (such as a table or view) is called an **Entity**. You don't need to extend any class, nor implement an interface to code an Entity. You don't even need XML descriptors for your mapping. Actually, the JPA is made up of annotations and only a few classes and interfaces. For example, we would mark the class Customer as Entity, as follows:

```
@Entity
public class Customer {
public Customer () { }

@Id
String name;

}
```

The preceding code snippet shows the minimal requirements for a class to be persistent. They are as follows:

- It must be identified as an entity by using the @javax.persistence.Entity annotation
- It must have an identifier attribute with the @javax.persistence.Id annotation
- It must have a no-argument constructor

The preceding Entity can be used to map a corresponding Customer object in your storage. For example, in order to insert a new customer you would just need to use a standard Java constructor of it, and use PersistenceContext to save it in your storage:

```
@Stateless
public class CustomerBean {

@PersistenceContext
private EntityManager em;

    public void createCustomer(String country,String name) {

        Customer customer = new Customer();
```

```
        customer.setCountry(country);
        customer.setName(name);
        em.persist(customer);
    }
}
```

Much the same way, you can query for entities using some specific JPA constructs such as `javax.persistence.Query` and a query language called JP-QL that translates object queries into database native queries:

```
public Customer findCustomerByName(String customerName) {

    Query query = em.createQuery("FROM Customer
where name=:name");
    query.setParameter("name", customerName);
    Customer customer = (Customer)query.getSingleResult();
    return customer;
}
```

The advantage of using a Persistence Layer API is that you don't write any specific database instructions, hence the preceding code can be used either to insert a query for rows in a relational database or new documents in a NoSQL database. The next sections will teach you how you can configure the Persistence Layer to use a MongoDB-compatible solution such as Hibernate OGM.

Entering Hibernate OGM

The JPA persistence engine used behind the scenes by WildFly is actually Hibernate, which cares for mapping database objects to Java entities. Although Hibernate has been designed around relational database mapping, a NoSQL version of it exists, which is called Hibernate OGM (`http://hibernate.org/ogm/`).

Hibernate OGM reuses Hibernate ORM's engine, but persists entities into a NoSQL data store instead of a relational database using the appropriate NoSQL driver.

The following figure describes the architecture of Hibernate OGM, showing its relation with the base Hibernate ORM framework:

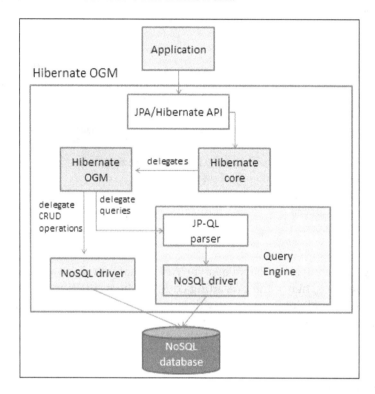

As you can see, the application layer interacts with the JPA (or Hibernate native) API. This layer uses the Hibernate ORM features contained in the Hibernate core implementation. In turn, the Hibernate core delegates the execution of queries and CRUD operations to Hibernate OGM.

As for queries, the query engine will drive the execution of JP-QL statements to the underlying storage. Other CRUD operations will be executed directly to the storage, with the mediation of your data store provider, which, in our case, uses the MongoDB driver.

The preceding concepts might look a bit abstract so we will provide a complete example of an application that uses some entities to store and retrieve documents in a MongoDB database.

Building a JPA project that uses Hibernate OGM

As most readers have some skills with Hibernate or JPA, we will reuse an example that was originally presented in an earlier book of mine (`https://www.packtpub.com/networking-and-servers/jboss-5-development`). The purpose of this exercise will be to demonstrate how you can apply a MongoDB storage to a standard application using Hibernate or JPA.

This example application simulates a simple online store where you can register new customers and add/issue new orders for each customer.

Here is the basic structure of our entity objects:

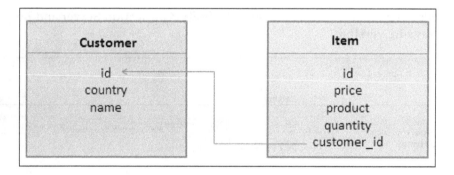

Now start NetBeans and from the **File** menu select **New Project**. Within the **Maven** categories, select **Web Application**. Click on **Next**. In the following window, enter the project name (for example, jpa-mongodb) and specify **GroupId**, **Version**, and **Package**, as we did in the previous chapter:

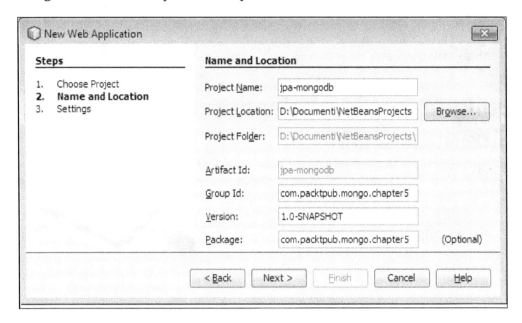

In the following window, select **Server** as **WildFly Application Server** and **Java EE 7 Web** as **Java EE version**:

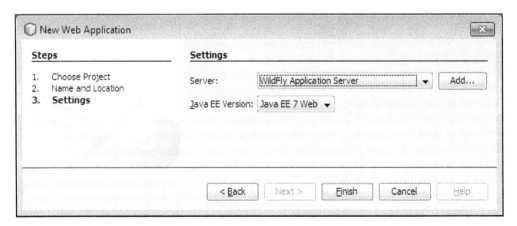

Click on **Finish** to create the Maven project.

Configuring the project dependencies

In order to compile your project, you will need to set up some dependencies in your pom.xml file. Start by including the **Bill of Materials (BoM)** for the WildFly application server and for Hibernate OGM:

```xml
<dependencyManagement>
  <dependencies>

    <dependency>
      <groupId>org.wildfly.bom</groupId>
      <artifactId>jboss-javaee-7.0-with-all</artifactId>
      <version>8.2.0.Final</version>
      <type>pom</type>
      <scope>import</scope>
    </dependency>

    <dependency>
      <groupId>org.hibernate.ogm</groupId>
      <artifactId>hibernate-ogm-bom</artifactId>
      <type>pom</type>
      <version>4.2.0.Beta1</version>
      <scope>import</scope>
    </dependency>

  </dependencies>
</dependencyManagement>
```

With the BoM in place, setting the actual dependencies used in the project will be simpler as we won't need to specify the actual version for the libraries to be used:

```xml
<dependencies>

  <dependency>
    <groupId>org.hibernate.ogm</groupId>
    <artifactId>hibernate-ogm-mongodb</artifactId>
  </dependency>

  <dependency>
    <groupId>javax.enterprise</groupId>
    <artifactId>cdi-api</artifactId>
    <scope>provided</scope>
  </dependency>
```

```
<dependency>
  <groupId>org.jboss.spec.javax.faces</groupId>
  <artifactId>jboss-jsf-api_2.2_spec</artifactId>
  <scope>provided</scope>
</dependency>

<dependency>
  <groupId>org.jboss.spec.javax.ejb</groupId>
  <artifactId>jboss-ejb-api_3.2_spec</artifactId>
  <scope>provided</scope>
</dependency>

<dependency>
  <groupId>org.jboss.spec.javax.annotation</groupId>
  <artifactId>jboss-annotations-api_1.2_spec</artifactId>
  <scope>provided</scope>
</dependency>

</dependencies>
```

Besides the standard Java EE API stack used to construct our application (CDI, JSF, JPA, and Annotations), we have included `org.hibernate.ogm` as well, which will be used to interact with MongoDB.

You can optionally include the Maven's WildFly plugin that can be used to deploy or undeploy our application directly from the Maven shell:

```
<build>
  <finalName>${project.artifactId}</finalName>
  <plugins>

    <plugin>
      <groupId>org.wildfly.plugins</groupId>
      <artifactId>wildfly-maven-plugin</artifactId>
      <version>1.0.2.Final</version>
    </plugin>
  </plugins>
</build>
```

Mapping the database collections

We will now add Java classes to our project, starting from the entities that will be in charge to map the database collections. Here is the `Customer` class, which stores all the records of the customers accessing our online store:

```
package com.packtpub.mongo.chapter5.model;

import javax.persistence.*;
import java.util.List;
import static javax.persistence.FetchType.EAGER;
import org.hibernate.annotations.GenericGenerator;

@Entity

public class Customer    {

    @Id
    @GeneratedValue(generator = "uuid")
    @GenericGenerator(name = "uuid", strategy = "uuid2")
    private String id;

    private String country;
    private String name;

    @OneToMany(mappedBy = "customerFK", fetch = EAGER)
    private List<Item> items;

    public Customer() {        }


    // Getter/Setters omitted for brevity
}
```

The first annotation we have added is @Entity, which declares the class as an entity.

 You can optionally include a @Table(name="yourtable") annotation at the class level to declare that the bean class uses a different name from the database collection.

The @Id annotation is mandatory; it describes the primary key of the table.

 If you need to use a composite primary key, then you can use @EmbeddedId, which denotes that more than one column behaves jointly as a primary key.

Along with @Id, there's the @GeneratedValue annotation. This is used to declare that the database is in charge of generating the value. @GenericGenerator is used to declare the strategy used for generating the ID, which in our case is a 128-bit unique identifier (UUID).

Moving along, we have included the fields of the entity, which map the corresponding keys of the customer. Finally, the @OneToMany annotation defines an association with one-to-many multiplicity.

Actually, the Customer class has many items. The corresponding orders are contained in a List collection.

 Within the @OneToMany annotation, we have chosen the EAGER attribute so that all the orders are populated at the same time when we issue a query on the Customer entity.

The second entity that we will include is the Item class, which contains all the items ordered by one customer. The code is as follows:

```
package com.packtpub.mongo.chapter5.model;

import javax.persistence.*;
import org.hibernate.annotations.GenericGenerator;

@Entity
public class Item   {

    @Id
    @GeneratedValue(generator = "uuid")
    @GenericGenerator(name = "uuid", strategy = "uuid2")
    private String id;

    private int price;

    private String product;

    private int quantity;

    @ManyToOne
    @JoinColumn(name = "CUSTOMER_ID")
    private Customer customerFK;
```

```
   public Item() {       }

   // Getters and Setters omitted for brevity
}
```

As you can see, the `Item` entity has the corresponding `@ManyToOne` annotation, which complements the `@OneToMany` relationship in the `Customer` class. `@JoinColumn` notifies the JPA engine that the `customerFK` field is mapped through the foreign key of the database `customer_id`.

Configuring persistence

The Entity API looks great and very intuitive; however, you might wonder how the server knows which database is supposed to store/query the `Entity` objects. The `persistence.xml` file is the standard JPA configuration file. Within this file, we will specify the persistence provider to be used for the database connection and the connection properties.

Create the following `persistence.xml` file under `src/main/resources` of your project:

```
<persistence version="2.0"
  xmlns="http://java.sun.com/xml/ns/persistence"
    xmlns:xsi="http://www.w3.org/2001/XMLSchema-instance"
      xsi:schemaLocation="http://java.sun.com/xml/ns/persistence
        http://java.sun.com/xml/ns/persistence/persistence_2_0.xsd">
  <persistence-unit name="mongo-ogm" transaction-type="JTA">
  <provider>org.hibernate.ogm.jpa.HibernateOgmPersistence</provider>
    <class>com.packtpub.mongo.chapter5.model.Customer</class>
    <class>com.packtpub.mongo.chapter5.model.Item</class>
    <properties>
      <property name="hibernate.transaction.jta.platform"
        value="org.hibernate.service.jta.platform.internal.
          JBossAppServerJtaPlatform"/>
      <property name="hibernate.ogm.datastore.database"
        value="javaee7"/>
      <property name="hibernate.ogm.datastore.host"
        value="localhost"/>
      <property name="hibernate.ogm.datastore.provider"
        value="MONGODB"/>
    </properties>
  </persistence-unit>
</persistence>
```

If you have been using JPA in some of your projects, you will notice an evident difference with the preceding `persistence.xml` file; as a matter of fact, there is no reference to the data source, which is the server resource used to provide connections to the `EntityManager` interface.

Instead, the data store connection is handled through the properties of the persistence provider, which is `org.hibernate.ogm.jpa.HibernateOgmPersistence`. The properties that we have configured are as follows:

- `hibernate.transaction.jta.platform`: This specifies the platform's Transaction API to be used when inserting/updating/deleting data
- `hibernate.ogm.datastore.database`: This specifies the database to be used, in our case, the MongoDB database
- `hibernate.ogm.datastore.host`: This specifies the host where the database is running
- `hibernate.ogm.datastore.provider`: This states the database provider; since we are connecting to MongoDB, our choice will be `MONGODB`

Coding the controller and EJB classes

Transactions are a fundamental part of every enterprise application; a common best practice is to use Enterprise Java Beans to perform database insert/update/delete operations as they are an inherently transactional component. In our case, transactions will be handled by the underlying JTA platform that is included in the application server.

For this purpose, we will add the `StoreManagerEJB` class, which contains all the CRUD operations that can be executed with the database:

```
package com.packtpub.mongo.chapter5.ejb;

import com.packtpub.mongo.chapter5.model.*;
import java.util.List;
import javax.ejb.Stateless;
import javax.persistence.EntityManager;
import javax.persistence.PersistenceContext;

import javax.persistence.Query;

@Stateless
public class StoreManagerEJB {

    @PersistenceContext(unitName = "mongo-ogm")
```

```
private EntityManager em;

public void createCustomer(String country, String name) {
  Customer customer = new Customer();
  customer.setCountry(country);
  customer.setName(name);
  em.persist(customer);
}

public void saveOrder(String idCustomer, int price,
  int quantity, String product) {
  Customer customer = findCustomerById(idCustomer);
  Item order = new Item();
  order.setCustomerFK(customer);
  order.setPrice(price);
  order.setQuantity(quantity);
  order.setProduct(product);
  em.persist(order);
}

public List<Item> findAllItems(String customerId) {
  Query query = em.createQuery("FROM Customer where id=:id");
  query.setParameter("id", customerId);
  Customer customer = (Customer) query.getSingleResult();
  List<Item> customerOrders = customer.getItems();
  return customerOrders;
}

public Customer findCustomerByName(String customerName) {
  Query query = em.createQuery("FROM Customer where
    name=:name");
  query.setParameter("name", customerName);
  Customer customer = (Customer) query.getSingleResult();
  return customer;
}

public Customer findCustomerById(String id) {
  Query query = em.createQuery("FROM Customer where id=:id");
  query.setParameter("id", id);
  Customer customer = (Customer) query.getSingleResult();
  return customer;
}
```

```
    public List<Customer> findAllCustomers() {
      Query query = em.createQuery("FROM Customer");
      List<Customer> customerList = query.getResultList();
      return customerList;
    }
}
```

The @PersistenceContext annotation added to the EntityManager field injects a container-managed persistence context. You might think of this as an object-oriented connection to the database.

The first method, createCustomer, shows you how to add a new customer to the database using JPA. As you can see, it's all about creating object instances. However, until you persist your objects, all the changes are held in the memory.

The method saveOrder works in quite the same way. Moving to the finder methods, we have coded a finder method for every business case so that we can query for all the items, customers, or a specific one, using a key as the filter. If you have already worked with Hibernate, the syntax used for queries should sound very familiar to you. In fact, JPA also uses a database-independent language, **Java Persistence Query Language (JP-QL)** to issues queries. It is a rich language that allows you to query any complex object's model (associations, inheritance, abstract classes, and so on) using common built-in database functions.

Hibernate OGM and JP-QL

The support for JP-QL constructs is still in the early stage of Hibernate OGM; therefore, right now, you cannot use all the constructs, which are available on RDBMS. In detail, the following constructs are allowed to be executed:

- Simple comparisons using "<", "!=", "=", ">=", and ">"
- IS NULL and IS NOT NULL
- The Boolean operators AND, OR, NOT
- LIKE, IN, and BETWEEN
- ORDER BY

On the other hand, the following are not supported:

- Cross entity joins as it's not possible to use joins in document-oriented databases such as MongoDB
- JP-QL functions in particular aggregation functions such as count, JP-QL update, and delete queries

Coding a controller bean

EJB classes cannot be directly exposed to our views; therefore, we need a component that acts as a controller for our application. We will add a CDI bean named `Manager` that will just be a wrapper between the view and the transactional layer (EJB). The source code of the `com.packtpub.mongo.chapter5.controller.Manager` class is as follows:

```java
package com.packtpub.mongo.chapter5.controller;

import java.util.*;

import javax.enterprise.inject.Model;
import javax.faces.application.FacesMessage;

import javax.faces.context.FacesContext;

import com.packtpub.mongo.chapter5.ejb.StoreManagerEJB;
import com.packtpub.mongo.chapter5.model.Customer;
import com.packtpub.mongo.chapter5.model.Item;
import javax.annotation.PostConstruct;

import javax.faces.event.ValueChangeEvent;
import javax.faces.model.SelectItem;
import javax.inject.Inject;

@Model
public class Manager    {

    @Inject
    StoreManagerEJB storeManager;

    private String customerId;
    private int orderQuantity;
    private int orderPrice;
    private String customerName;
    private String customerCountry;
    private String orderProduct;

    List<Item> listOrders;
    List<SelectItem> listCustomers;
```

```java
public Manager() {    }

@PostConstruct
public void init() {
  getListCustomers();
  if (listCustomers.size() > 0) {
    customerId = listCustomers.get(0).getValue().toString();
    listOrders = storeManager.findAllItems(customerId);
  }
}

public void findAllCustomers() {
  List<Customer> listCustomersEJB =
    storeManager.findAllCustomers();
  for (Customer customer : listCustomersEJB) {
    listCustomers.add(new SelectItem(customer.getId(),
      customer.getName()));
  }
}

public void createCustomer() {
  storeManager.createCustomer(customerCountry, customerName);
  FacesMessage fm = new FacesMessage("Created Customer" +
    customerName + " from " + customerCountry);
  FacesContext.getCurrentInstance().addMessage("Message", fm);
  customerName = null;
  customerCountry = null;
  listCustomers = null;
}

public void saveOrder() {
  storeManager.saveOrder(customerId, orderPrice, orderQuantity,
    orderProduct);
  FacesMessage fm = new FacesMessage("Saved order for" +
    orderQuantity + " of " + orderProduct + " and customer " +
      customerId);
  FacesContext.getCurrentInstance().addMessage("Message", fm);
  orderPrice = 0;
  orderQuantity = 0;
  orderProduct = null;
}

public void changeListener(ValueChangeEvent e) {
  Object oldValue = e.getNewValue();
  customerId = e.getNewValue().toString();
```

```
    listOrders = storeManager.findAllItems(customerId);
  }

  public List<SelectItem> getListCustomers() {
    if (listCustomers == null) {
      listCustomers = new ArrayList();
      findAllCustomers();
    }
    return listCustomers;
  }

  // Getter-Setters omitted for brevity
}
```

The `Manager` class exposes two main collections to the view: a collection named `listCustomers`, which displays the list of customers in a combobox, and a collection of named `listOrders`, which contains the orders placed by each customer.

Within the `init` method (annotated with `@PostConstruct`, thus invoked after the creation of the class) the two collections are loaded and displayed.

The `findAllCustomers` method is used to load the list of customers using the EJB's `findAllCustomers` method.

Then, the `createCustomer` method wraps the creation of a new customer using the EJB's corresponding `createCustomer` method.

The method `saveOrder` wraps the execution of the `saveOrder` method of the `StoreManagerEJB` class.

Finally, a `changeListener` method is included to automatically reload the list of orders as soon as a customer is selected from the combobox.

> The class includes the `Customer` and `Item` fields as well, which are used to transport the information from the HTML page to `Manager`. You can further optimize the above code by using CDI producers to expose the items and their collections via EL expressions.

Coding the views

This application is made up of three views, one for each use case:

- An `index.xhtml` page that contains the main screen and is loaded at startup
- A `newCustomer.xhtml` page that is used to add a new customer

- A `newOrder.xhtml` page that can be used to place a new order for an item by a specific customer

Let's see each page in detail.

The main view

The `index.xhtml` page contains a form with the list of customers and their orders:

```
<!DOCTYPE html PUBLIC "-//W3C//DTD XHTML 1.0 Transitional//EN"
  "http://www.w3.org/TR/xhtml1/DTD/xhtml1-transitional.dtd">
<html xmlns="http://www.w3.org/1999/xhtml"
  xmlns:h="http://java.sun.com/jsf/html"
    xmlns:f="http://java.sun.com/jsf/core"
      xmlns:c="http://java.sun.com/jsp/jstl/core">
  <h:head>
    <style type="text/css">
      @import url("css/store.css");
    </style>
  </h:head>

  <h:body>
    <h:panelGrid columns="1" border="1" styleClass="spring">
      <f:facet name="header">
        <h:outputText value="Order List"/>
      </f:facet>
      <h:form id="listOrdersForm">
        <h:outputText value="Select Customer:" />
        <h:selectOneMenu id="selectCustomer"
          valueChangeListener="#{manager.changeListener}"
            onchange="submit()"    value="#{manager.customerId}"
              styleClass="buttons">
          <f:selectItems value="#{manager.listCustomers}" />

        </h:selectOneMenu>

        <h:dataTable value="#{manager.listOrders}"
          var="orders" border="1" rowClasses="row1, row2"
            headerClass="header">
        <h:column>
          <f:facet name="header">
            <h:outputText value="Product" />
          </f:facet>
        <h:outputText value="#{orders.product}" />
          </h:column>
          <h:column>
```

```
        <f:facet name="header">
    <h:outputText value="Price" />
      </f:facet>
    <h:outputText value="#{orders.price}" />
      </h:column>
      <h:column>

        <f:facet name="header">
    <h:outputText value="Quantity" />
      </f:facet>
    <h:outputText value="#{orders.quantity}" />
      </h:column>
      </h:dataTable>
      <h:commandButton action="newCustomer" value="Insert
        Customer" styleClass="buttons" />
      <h:commandButton action="newOrder" value="Insert Order"
        styleClass="buttons" />
    </h:form>
  </h:panelGrid>
  <h:messages style="color:red;margin:8px;" />

  </h:body>
</html>
```

We have highlighted the two most interesting sections:

- The first block, which renders a combobox, is used to display the list of customers. The list is maintained in the listCustomers collection of the Manager bean. SelectItem registers a valueChangeListener each time the selection is changed, triggering the method changeListener of the Manager class.

- The second block is used to display the orders of each customer in a tabular way. The data of this collection is maintained in the listOrders collection of the Manager bean.

At the bottom of the view, a pair of buttons is used to navigate to the other views of the application, which are described in the next sections.

The newCustomer view

The newCustomer.xhtml file is a form that fills up the properties required to insert a new customer. Here is the core part of it:

```
<h:panelGrid columns="1" border="1" styleClass="spring">
  <f:facet name="header">
```

```
      <h:outputText value="New Customer"/>
  </f:facet>
  <h:form id="newCustomer">
    <h:panelGrid columns="2" border="1" styleClass="spring">
      <f:facet name="header">
        <h:outputText value="Insert new Customer" />
      </f:facet>
      <h:outputText value="Name" />
      <h:inputText value="#{manager.customerName}" />
      <h:outputText value="Country" />
      <h:inputText value="#{manager.customerCountry}" />
      <h:commandButton action="#{manager.createCustomer}"
        value="Insert Customer" />
      <h:commandButton action="index" value="Back" />
    </h:panelGrid>

  </h:form>
</h:panelGrid>
<h:messages style="color:red;margin:8px;" />
```

The highlighted button, when clicked, executes the createCustomer method of the Manager bean, thus inserting a new customer into the database.

The newOrder view

The last view of our application is newOrder.xhtml, which adds a new order for a selected customer:

```
<h:panelGrid columns="1" border="1" styleClass="spring">
  <f:facet name="header">
    <h:outputText value="New Order"/>
  </f:facet>
  <h:form id="newOrder">
    <h:panelGrid columns="2" border="1" styleClass="spring">
      <f:facet name="header">
        <h:outputText value="Insert new Order" />
      </f:facet>
      <h:outputText value="Product" />
      <h:inputText value="#{manager.orderProduct}" />
      <h:outputText value="Quantity" />
      <h:inputText value="#{manager.orderQuantity}" />
      <h:outputText value="Price" />
      <h:inputText value="#{manager.orderPrice}" />
      <h:outputText value="Customer" />
```

```
<h:selectOneMenu id="selectCustomerforOrder"
        value="#{manager.customerId}">
  <f:selectItems value="#{manager.listCustomers}" />
</h:selectOneMenu>
<h:commandButton action="#{manager.saveOrder}"
        value="Save Order" />
  <h:commandButton action="index" value="Back" />
</h:panelGrid>

</h:form>
</h:panelGrid>
<h:messages style="color:red;margin:8px;" />
```

Again, Manager is in charge of inserting the saved order into the database when the user clicks on the **Save Order** button.

Compiling and running the example

You can compile, package, and deploy your application by simply right-clicking on the project icon and choosing **Run**.

If you want to manage the above tasks from the shell, you can issue the following Maven goals, provided that you have installed the Maven's WildFly plugin (see *Chapter 4, MongoDB in the Java EE 7 Enterprise Environment,* for more information about configuring your pom.xml file):

mvn clean install wildfly:deploy

The home page (index.html) will initially display a blank list of customers and items:

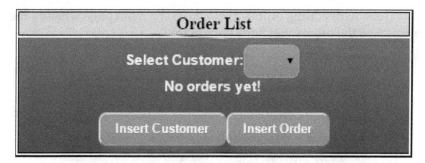

Click on the **Insert Customer** button at first, which will take you to the
`newOrder.xhtml` view where you can register a new customer into your store:

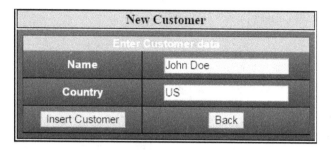

With a customer available, click on the **Back** button to return to the home page. From
there, add a new order by clicking on the **Insert Order** button, which will take you to
the `newOrder.xhtml` page:

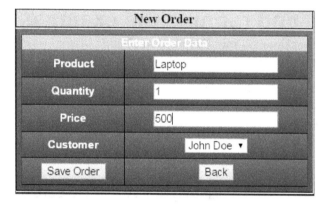

Once you're done with adding orders, check from the main page whether the
customer contains the orders that have been placed:

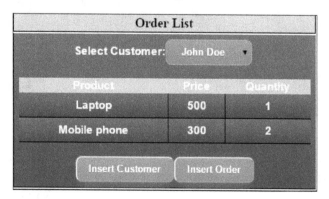

A look into MongoDB

So far, we have handled database interaction just using the JPA API; as a matter of fact, we didn't write even a MongoDB query or insert it into our code. Believe it or not, the collections and documents have been properly inserted into our database and checking it takes just a minute.

First, from the mongo shell, enter into the `javaee7` database and run the following command:

```
C:\>mongo
MongoDB shell version: 2.6.4
connecting to: test
> use javaee7
switched to db javaee7
```

Now, let's have a look at the collections that are available:

```
> show collections
Customer
Item
. . . .
system.indexes
```

You will find, among the other collections, that the customer and item collections have been created. With the following query, we will verify that the content of the collections is consistent with the data, which has just been inserted into the application:

```
> db.Customer.find().pretty()
{
  "_id" : "c5878f45-d472-48cb-8ff1-0efc62dca9fb",
  "name" : "John Doe",
  "country" : "US",
  "items" : [
    "6295d5e1-fec9-4035-8214-047975e45acb",
    "1af91459-1c24-4592-a160-694125229683"
  ]
}
> db.Item.find().pretty()
{
```

```
  "_id" : "6295d5e1-fec9-4035-8214-047975e45acb",

  "product" : "Laptop",

  "price" : 500,

  "quantity" : 1,

  "CUSTOMER_ID" : "c5878f45-d472-48cb-8ff1-0efc62dca9fb"
}
{

  "_id" : "1af91459-1c24-4592-a160-694125229683",

  "product" : "Mobile phone",

  "price" : 300,

  "quantity" : 2,

  "CUSTOMER_ID" : "c5878f45-d472-48cb-8ff1-0efc62dca9fb"
}
```

Using native queries in your Hibernate OGM

If you want to use the raw power of MongoDB queries within your Hibernate OGM applications, then this is possible as well. This can be a good choice if you feel too limited by the current Hibernate OGM JP-QL. On the other hand, you have to consider that you will lose portability of your application, in case you change the database.

In JPA, you can use the `EntityManager.createNativeQuery` method to execute a native query. You can also use a `Named` query to define your queries apart from your business methods.

Let's see an example of it:

```
public List<Customer> queryNative() {

    String query1 = "db.Customer.find({'country': 'US'})";
    Query query = em.createNativeQuery(query1, Customer.class);

    List<Customer> list = query.getResultList();
    return list;
}
```

The preceding `Native` query executes a find on the `Customer` collection, by filtering through the customers that have the `country` key as equals to `US`.

The preceding query can also be expressed by using the `NamedQuery` interface, which can be attached to the `Customer` entity as follows:

```
@Entity
@NamedNativeQuery(
name = "USCustomers",
query = "db.Customer.find({'country': 'US'})",
resultClass = Customer.class )

public class Customer    {

. . . .
}
```

You can then execute the native named query from within your code as follows:

```
List<Customer> list = em.createNamedQuery( "USCustomers",
  Customer.class ).getResultList();
```

Summary

In this chapter, we have gone through the Hibernate OGM framework showing how to deal with a NoSQL database such as MongoDB without writing database-specific instructions. This provides a great benefit in terms of abstractions and uses a standard specification called JPA to simplify the development of your applications.

Other valuable frameworks to simplify the interaction with MongoDB do exist; we have selected one more, named Spring Data MongoDB, which is a project under the umbrella of the popular Spring framework. We'll see more of this in the next chapter.

6

Building Applications for MongoDB with Spring Data

In this chapter, we will learn how to develop Java applications with MongoDB from another perspective. The framework we will use is Spring Boot, which offers a new paradigm for developing applications based on the Spring core framework. In particular, we will learn how to store data on MongoDB by means of the Spring Data project. Here is the list of the topics discussed in this chapter:

- An introduction to Spring Boot and the Spring Data framework
- Constructing a Spring Boot application using the repository interface
- Using the Mongo template interface to achieve fine grained control of MongoDB

Introducing Spring Boot

The Spring framework is the leading Java/JEE application framework. It is a valid alternative to the standard Java EE programming model and provides a lightweight container and a non-invasive API enabled by the use of dependency injection, portable service abstractions, and aspect-oriented programming.

Although Spring is a lightweight framework in terms of programming code, it does require a complex configuration, which represents an obstacle for quickly developing applications. As a matter of fact, the developers should concentrate on the business logic rather than dealing with configuration concerns.

The most exciting thing that has happened in the last few years in the Spring arena is the development of a project called **Spring Boot**, which offers a new paradigm for developing Spring applications with more agility while focusing on your business methods rather than the thought of configuring Spring itself.

Getting started with Spring Boot

Spring Boot does not require complex configuration files as it is able to discover classes by looking in the classpath of your applications and building a single runnable JAR of it, which makes it convenient to make your service portable too.

Let's see a practical example of it:

```
package hello;
import org.springframework.stereotype.Component;

@Component
public class SimpleBean
{
  @Override
  public String toString() {
    return "Hello , This is an example component";
  }
}
```

The preceding class contains a `@Component` annotation, which marks a Java class as a bean so the component-scanning mechanism of Spring can pick it up and pull it into the application context. We will now code a minimal Spring Boot application, which will be able to discover the class with as little as a single annotation:

```
import org.springframework.beans.factory.annotation.Autowired;
import org.springframework.boot.CommandLineRunner;

import org.springframework.boot.SpringApplication;
import
  org.springframework.boot.autoconfigure.SpringBootApplication;

@SpringBootApplication
public class Application implements CommandLineRunner {

    @Autowired
    SimpleBean bean;

    public static void main(String[] args) {
        SpringApplication.run(Application.class, args);

    }

    @Override
    public void run(String... args) throws Exception {
```

```
        System.out.println("Found bean:" + bean);
    }
}
```

This class, although very simple, contains lots of things in it. Inside it, we have used `@SpringBootApplication` to leverage a set of functionalities, which are commonly required by most Spring applications:

- The `@Configuration` annotation identifies the class as a source of bean definitions for the application context.

- The `@EnableAutoConfiguration` annotation enables Spring Boot to add beans based on the application's classpath, and various property settings.

- The `@ComponentScan` annotation tells Spring to look for other beans, configurations, and services in the same package as your application class so that you will be able to find the `SimpleBean` class.

- Finally, `@EnableWebMvc` flags the application as a web application and thus activates the component called `DispatcherServlet` to capture HTTP requests.

All the preceding functionalities are automatically included once you provide the `@SpringBootAnnotation` within your class.

The `main` method contained in the class uses Spring Boot's `SpringApplication.run` method to launch an application and print the `toString` method of `SimpleBean` class. Although nothing fancy happens here, we have coded a Spring application without writing a single line of XML and we could have easily added some functionalities such as querying data from a storage or a REST controller with little effort. Providing an example of this requires an introduction to the Spring Data project, which can be easily combined into the Spring Boot container providing integration with relational databases and NoSQL solutions such as MongoDB.

Getting started with Spring Data

Implementing a data access layer of an application has traditionally been a pain point for developers. The critical points are that too much boilerplate code has to be written and the resulting domain classes are not designed in a real object-oriented or domain-driven style.

Spring Data is a high-level Spring project whose purpose is to unify and simplify the access to different kinds of persistence stores, reducing the amount of boilerplate code to be written, and providing common patterns that can be applied to relational database systems and NoSQL data stores.

The following figure gives you a bird's eye view of the Spring Data framework:

As you can see from the preceding figure, two core instruments can be used to access a MongoDB storage:

- A **MongoRepository** interface acts as a marker place to capture the document model, thus, providing a convenient way to derive DB statements directly from the field name of your documents.

- A template interface called **MongoTemplate** is a high-level abstraction for storing and querying documents and its super interface called MongoOperations. You will find this approach familiar if you have been using the JDBC support in the Spring framework.

The upcoming section will introduce the core concepts of both instruments with some proof of concept examples of interaction with MongoDB.

Using the Spring repository to access MongoDB

The `org.springframework.data.repository.Repository` interface is a core part of the Spring Data framework. This interface acts as a marker interface to capture the domain type to manage, as well as the domain type's ID type. So, the purpose of the interface is to hold type information, as well as being able to discover interfaces that extend this one during classpath scanning.

The advantage of implementing the repository in your code is that you will be able to expose CRUD methods for your data storage by simply declaring methods with the same signature as those exposed in the `org.springframework.data.repository.CrudRepository` interface. This allows a drastic reduction of boiler plate code to write the most common functionalities required by your applications.

We will now provide a proof of concept example of a Spring Boot application using Spring Data for MongoDB to perform common CRUD operations.

Coding our Spring Boot application

Our project will be a simple Maven-based Java application, which includes as first class the `Book` class, which will map a corresponding MongoDB document. Start by navigating to **New | Maven | Java application** from the **File** menu and select `com.packtpub.mongo.chapter6` as the package's base directory.

Next, we will configure `pom.xml`, so that you will be able to compile and deploy our application:

```
<project xmlns="http://maven.apache.org/POM/4.0.0"
  xmlns:xsi="http://www.w3.org/2001/XMLSchema-instance"
    xsi:schemaLocation="http://maven.apache.org/POM/4.0.0
      http://maven.apache.org/xsd/maven-4.0.0.xsd">
  <modelVersion>4.0.0</modelVersion>
  <groupId>com.packtpub.mongo.chapter6</groupId>
  <artifactId>spring-mongodb</artifactId>
  <version>1.0-SNAPSHOT</version>
  <packaging>jar</packaging>
  <properties>
    <project.build.sourceEncoding>UTF-
      8</project.build.sourceEncoding>
    <maven.compiler.source>1.7</maven.compiler.source>
    <maven.compiler.target>1.7</maven.compiler.target>
  </properties>

  <parent>
    <groupId>org.springframework.boot</groupId>
    <artifactId>spring-boot-starter-parent</artifactId>
    <version>1.2.3.RELEASE</version>
  </parent>

  <dependencies>
    <dependency>
      <groupId>org.springframework.boot</groupId>
      <artifactId>spring-boot-starter-data-mongodb</artifactId>
```

```xml
        </dependency>
    </dependencies>

    <build>
      <plugins>
        <plugin>
          <groupId>org.springframework.boot</groupId>
          <artifactId>spring-boot-maven-plugin</artifactId>
        </plugin>
      </plugins>
    </build>

    <repositories>
      <repository>
        <id>spring-releases</id>
        <name>Spring Releases</name>
        <url>https://repo.spring.io/libs-release</url>
      </repository>
    </repositories>
    <pluginRepositories>
      <pluginRepository>
        <id>spring-releases</id>
        <name>Spring Releases</name>
        <url>https://repo.spring.io/libs-release</url>
      </pluginRepository>
    </pluginRepositories>
</project>
```

As you can see from the preceding highlighted sections, the simplest way to compile and build a Spring Boot project consists in including in your pom.xml a starter POMs that references the Spring Boot Parent. We have then added a dependency to Spring Data MongoDB artifacts and a plugin to execute Spring Boot from Maven.

Mapping Java classes with Spring Data

Mapping a Java class with a MongoDB document is straightforward, as the built-in MongoMappingConverter will do most of the job for you. At minimum, you need to provide an org.springframework.data.mongodb.core.mapping.Document annotation to your class to candidate it for mapping the class to a MongoDB document:

```java
package com.packtpub.mongo.chapter6.repository;

import org.springframework.data.annotation.Id;
```

```
import org.springframework.data.mongodb.core.mapping.Document;

@Document
public class Book {

  @Id
  private String id;
  private String title;
  private String author;
  private int price;
  private String type;

  @Override
  public String toString() {
    return "Book{" + "id=" + id + ", title=" + title + ", author="
      + author + ", price=" + price+"}";
  }

  public Book(String title, String author, String type, int price)
  {
    this.title = title;
    this.author = author;
    this.price = price;
    this.type = type;
  }

    // Getters/Setters omitted for brevity
}
```

Within this class, the @Id annotation tells the mapper, which property you want to use for the _id property of MongoDB. You can customize the behavior of MongoMappingConverter by providing a custom name for your Mongo documents, as shown in the following code:

```
@Document(collection = "mybooks")
public class Book {

  . . .
}
```

You can also customize the mapping between the fields and the database keys by using the @Field annotation as shown in the following code:

```
@Field("booktitle")
private String title;
```

Having built the model, we will now concentrate on the `Repository` class. Our repository class will extend the `org.springframework.data.mongodb.repository.MongoRepository` interface, plugging the types required by our model: `Book` and `String`:

```
package com.packtpub.mongo.chapter6.repository;
import java.util.List;
import
  org.springframework.data.mongodb.repository.MongoRepository;

public interface BookRepository extends MongoRepository<Book,
  String> {

  public Book findByTitle(String title);
  public List<Book> findByType(String type);
  public List<Book> findByAuthor(String author);

}
```

Within this interface, we already have many standard CRUD operations (Create-Read-Update-Delete) out of the box, but we can define other queries as needed by simply declaring their method signature. In our case, we have added finder methods for specific attributes of our `Book` class such as `findByTile`, `findByType`, and `findByAuthor`.

The advantage of using this approach is two-fold:

- You will write the least amount of code to perform CRUD operations
- You don't need to use the database-specific language to perform those operations

We can wire up our application by adding a Spring Boot application class, which will execute some CRUD operations by using the `BookRepository` class.

Here is our `Application` class:

```
package com.packtpub.mongo.chapter6.repository;

import org.springframework.beans.factory.annotation.Autowired;
import org.springframework.boot.CommandLineRunner;
import org.springframework.boot.SpringApplication;
import org.springframework.boot.autoconfigure.SpringBootApplication;

@SpringBootApplication
public class Application implements CommandLineRunner {
```

```
@Autowired
private  BookRepository repository;

public static void main(String[] args) {
  SpringApplication.run(Application.class, args);
}

@Override
public void run(String... args) throws Exception {

  repository.deleteAll();
  System.out.println("Collection deleted");

  repository.save(new  Book("A Tale Of Two Cities", "Charles
    Dickens","Novel", 10));
  repository.save(new  Book("The Da Vinci Code", "Dan Brown",
    "thriller", 12));
  repository.save(new  Book("Think and Grow Rich", "Napoleon
    Hill","Motivational", 10));
  repository.save(new  Book("The Hobbit", "J.R.R. Tolkien",
    "Fantasy", 8));
  repository.save(new Book("Le Petit Prince", "Antoine de
    Saint-Exupery","Novel", 8));

  System.out.println("Book found with findAll():");
  System.out.println("-----------------------------");
  for ( Book bstore : repository.findAll()) {
    System.out.println(bstore);
  }
  System.out.println();


  System.out.println("Book found with findByTitle('The Da Vinci
    Code'):");
  System.out.println("-----------------------------");
  Book book1 = repository.findByTitle("The Da Vinci Code");
  book1.setPrice(5);
  // Update Book
  repository.save(book1);

  book1 = repository.findByTitle("The Da Vinci Code");
  System.out.println(book1);

  // Delete Book
```

```
        repository.delete(book1);

        System.out.println("Book found with findByType('Novel'):");
        System.out.println("------------------------------");
        for ( Book book : repository.findByType("Novel")) {
          System.out.println(book);
        }

    }
}
```

Our SpringBootApplication class implements the `CommandLineRunner` interface so that the `run` method of the class will be invoked automatically when when the application starts.

Thanks to `@SpringBootAnnotation`, we will be able to inject into our class the `BookRepository` interface and the methods contained in it.

We start by using the `deleteAll` method, which is inherited from `MongoRepository`, so that we start with a clean collection of books.

Then we add some books to our collection using the `save` method on instances of the `Book` class.

 The `save` method, by definition, is supposed to update an object in the `upsert` style, that is, update if present and insert if not.

The next method, `findAll`, is executed to return the list of books as proof that we managed to store them correctly.

The `findByTitle` method demonstrates how to use a method defined in our `BookRepository` class to search for a specific book. The book is then updated using the `save` method and finally deleted by the built-in `delete` method available in the `Repository` interface.

Finally, the `findByType` method is executed to return a collection of books of a particular type.

Running the example

Having included the Spring Boot plugin in your `pom.xml` file, it will be fairly simple to run and test your application. You can run it by using the following command:

mvn spring-boot:run

As an alternative, you can simply right-click on NetBeans and choose **Run File**.

The expected output will inform us that the books have been created and the finder queries will show the single books or the collection of books queried, as shown in the following code:

```
Collection deleted
Book found with findAll():
--------------------------------
Book{id=55643737438717ca06d80b8e, title=A Tale Of Two Cities,
author=Charles Dickens, price=10}
Book{id=55643737438717ca06d80b8f, title=The Da Vinci Code, author=Dan
Brown, price=12}
Book{id=55643737438717ca06d80b90, title=Think and Grow Rich,
author=Napoleon Hill, price=10}
Book{id=55643737438717ca06d80b91, title=The Hobbit, author=J.R.R.
Tolkien, price=8}
Book{id=55643737438717ca06d80b92, title=Le Petit Prince,
author=Antoine de Saint-Exupery, price=8}
Book found with findByTitle('The Da Vinci Code'):
--------------------------------
Book{id=55643737438717ca06d80b8f, title=The Da Vinci Code, author=Dan
Brown, price=5}
Book found with findByType('Novel'):
--------------------------------
Book{id=55643737438717ca06d80b8e, title=A Tale Of Two Cities,
author=Charles Dickens, price=10}
Book{id=55643737438717ca06d80b92, title=Le Petit Prince,
author=Antoine de Saint-Exupery, price=8}
```

As proof of concept, you can connect to the Mongo shell and execute a `find` on the book collection to check whether the data matches with your output, using the following code:

```
db.book.find()
```

Customizing the repository storage

Our simple application stored our collection of books on the default database host, using the `test` database. This is obviously not what you would need in a real application. Luckily, it is not difficult to customize the settings used by the `Repository` class. You can do it by extending `org.springframework.data.mongodb.config.AbstractMongoConfiguration` and implementing the methods required for connecting to MongoDB:

```
package com.packtpub.mongo.chapter6.repository;

import com.mongodb.Mongo;
```

```
import com.mongodb.MongoClient;
import org.springframework.context.annotation.Configuration;
import org.springframework.data.mongodb.config.
    AbstractMongoConfiguration;
import org.springframework.data.mongodb.repository.config.
    EnableMongoRepositories;

@Configuration
@EnableMongoRepositories
public class MongoConfiguration extends AbstractMongoConfiguration
  {

    @Override
    protected String getDatabaseName() {
      return "springdata";
    }

    @Override
    public Mongo mongo() throws Exception {
      return new MongoClient("127.0.0.1", 27017);
    }

    @Override
    protected String getMappingBasePackage() {
      return "com.packtpub.mongo.chapter6.repository";
    }
  }
```

In the preceding example, we will connect to the springdata database available on 127.0.0.1. The @EnableMongoRepositories annotation is used to activate the MongoDB repositories — by specifying the mapping base package; it will trigger scanning of the package of annotated classes.

Using JSON queries in your repository classes

When using the MongoRepository interface, you can still use the raw power of JSON queries to perform custom query operations on your data. This can be achieved by adding the org.springframework.data.mongodb.repository.Query annotation on the repository finder methods. This allows specifying a MongoDB JSON query string instead of having the query derived from the method name. Consider the following example:

```
public interface BookRepository extends MongoRepository<Book,
   String> {

   @Query("{ 'type' : ?0 }")
   public List<Book> findByBookType(String type);
   @Query("{ 'type' : {$ne : ?0} }")
   public List<Book> findByBookTypeNot(String type);

}
```

In the above repository class, we have added two methods, the first one
(findByBookType) will execute a JSON finder query on books of a certain type. The
second one (findByBookTypeNot) will instead return books, which are not of the
same type as the first one.

In the *Creating fine grained queries using Criteria* section, we will discuss more in depth
about using the Query interface with the Criteria class, to create complex searches.

Serving MongoDB using Spring REST

A Spring Boot application includes out-of-the-box web capabilities. In particular,
a DispatcherServlet class is available to serve the content created in your
application. A practical use of it is creating an HTTP REST interface to access
the content of your repository.

In order to use Spring REST annotations in your code, you need at first to include its
dependency in the pom.xml file:

```
<dependency>
   <groupId>org.springframework.boot</groupId>
   <artifactId>spring-boot-starter-data-rest</artifactId>
</dependency>
```

Next, we can move to the code; by adding an annotation to our repository class
named @RepositoryRestResource, we can specify the resource path for our REST
resource:

```
package com.packtpub.mongo.chapter6.repository;

import java.util.List;

import org.springframework.data.mongodb.repository.MongoRepository;
import org.springframework.data.repository.query.Param;
```

```
import org.springframework.data.rest.core.annotation.
RepositoryRestResource;

@RepositoryRestResource(collectionResourceRel = "book", path =
  "book")
public interface BookRepository extends MongoRepository<Book, String>
{

  public Book findByTitle(@Param("title") String title);
  public List<Book> findByType(@Param("type") String type);
  public List<Book> findByAuthor(@Param("author") String author);
}
```

At execution time, Spring Data REST will create an implementation
of our BookRepository interface automatically. Then it will use the
@RepositoryRestResource annotation to direct Spring MVC to create
RESTful endpoints available on the URI path /book.

> Each of the methods contained in the interface are accepting a Param,
> which is used as a filter by the query.

When executing the Spring application class, an embedded web server will start.
As our collection of books has been bound to the /book URI, let's request the URL
http://localhost:8080/book.

Here is the expected output from the browser or the tool you have used to perform
the request (the full output has been shortened for brevity):

```
http://localhost:8080/book
{
  "_links" : {
    "self" : {
      "href" : "http://localhost:8080/book{?page,size,sort}",
      "templated" : true
    },
    "search" : {
      "href" : "http://localhost:8080/book/search"
    }
  },
  "_embedded" : {
    "book" : [ {
      "title" : "A Tale Of Two Cities",
      "author" : "Charles Dickens",
      "price" : 10,
      "type" : "Novel",
```

```
    "_links" : {
      "self" : {
        "href" :
          "http://localhost:8080/book/55644f4b438730fc13627847"
      }
    }
  },
    .  .  .
  "page" : {
    "size" : 20,
    "totalElements" : 4,
    "totalPages" : 1,
    "number" : 0
  }
}
```

As you can see, Spring REST used JSON **Hypertext Application Language** (HAL) to render the response. HAL defines links to be contained in a _link property of the returned document.

By issuing a request to the root URL under which the Spring Data REST application is deployed, the client can extract a set of links from the returned JSON object that represents the next level of resources that are available to the client.

By adding the search pattern to our URI (http://localhost:8080/book/search), we will discover the find methods that are available:

```
{
  "_links" : {
    "findByType" : {
      "href" : "http://localhost:8080/book/search/findByType{?type}",
      "templated" : true
    },
    "findByAuthor" : {
      "href" : "http://localhost:8080/book/search/
findByAuthor{?author}",
      "templated" : true
    },
    "findByTitle" : {
      "href" : "http://localhost:8080/book/search/
findByTitle{?title}",
      "templated" : true
    }
  }
}
```

From there, you can query individual search methods such as `http://localhost:8080/book/search/findByType?type=Novel` that will return as expected:

```
{
    "_embedded" : {
        "book" : [ {
            "title" : "A Tale Of Two Cities",
            "author" : "Charles Dickens",
            "price" : 10,
            "type" : "Novel",
            "_links" : {
                "self" : {
                    "href" : "http://localhost:8080/
book/55644f4b438730fc13627847"
                }
            }
        }, {
            "title" : "Le Petit Prince",
            "author" : "Antoine de Saint-Exupery",
            "price" : 8,
            "type" : "Novel",
            "_links" : {
                "self" : {
                    "href" : "http://localhost:8080/
book/55644f4b438730fc1362784b"
                }
            }
        } ]
    }
}
```

Obviously, the GET calls are not the only option that is available. You can also issue a POST to insert a new document, PUT to replace it, PATCH to update it, or DELETE, which deletes an existing record.

For example, the following POST executed with `curl` will add a new book to our collection:

```
curl -i -X POST -H "Content-Type:application/json" -d '{    "title" :
"Lord of the Rings","author" : "J.R.R. Tolkien","price" : 10,"type" :
"Fantasy" }' http://localhost:8080/book
```

Using the Mongo template component to access MongoDB

Using the repository interface provides a convenient way to create applications using standard CRUD operations, which are prebuilt around the fields contained in the model. If you need fine grained control over your data, an alternative is to use MongoTemplate, which is located in the package org.springframework.data.document.mongodb.

The simplest way to use MongoTemplate is to wire the MongoOperations component in your code, which is the superinterface of MongoTemplate. This interface replicates the methods that are already available in the Mongo driver, thus making the transition simpler between the driver and MongoTemplate. For example, you can execute methods such as find, findOne, findAndModify, save, insert, update, and remove. The major difference between the Mongo driver and MongoOperations is that the latter uses the domain objects instead of DBObject and that it includes fluent APIs for the Query, Criteria, and Update operations instead of using DBObject to specify the parameters for those operations.

In the next section, we will show how to build a simple application, starting from a **Data Access Object (DAO)** layer, which will use the MongoOperations interface to wrap the required CRUD methods on the database.

Building up the data access layer

The DAO layer is used to abstract access to data sources, thus making your applications portable between different database vendors. We will start by coding an interface for our DAO, which will encapsulate the core methods of our application:

```
public interface BookDAO {

    public void insert(Book p);
    public void insertAll(Book[] p);
    public Book findByTitle(String id);

    public void update(Book p);

    public int deleteByTitle(String id);
    public void dropCollectionIfExist();
}
```

The implementation class, which is tagged with the @Repository annotation is as follows:

```
package com.packtpub.mongo.chapter6.template;

import org.springframework.data.mongodb.core.MongoOperations;
import org.springframework.data.mongodb.core.query.Criteria;
import org.springframework.data.mongodb.core.query.Query;

import com.mongodb.WriteResult;
import java.util.Arrays;
import org.springframework.beans.factory.annotation.Autowired;
import org.springframework.stereotype.Repository;

@Repository
public class BookDAOImpl  implements BookDAO {

  @Autowired
  private MongoOperations mongoOps;

  private static final String BOOK_COLLECTION = "Book";

  public BookDAOImpl(MongoOperations mongoOps) {
    this.mongoOps = mongoOps;
  }

  public BookDAOImpl() {     }

  public void dropCollectionIfExist() {

    if (mongoOps.collectionExists(BOOK_COLLECTION)) {
      mongoOps.dropCollection(BOOK_COLLECTION);
      System.out.println("dropped collection");
    }
  }


  public void insert(Book p) {
    this.mongoOps.insert(p, BOOK_COLLECTION);
  }

  public void insertAll(Book[] books) {
    mongoOps.insert(Arrays.asList(books), BOOK_COLLECTION);
```

```
    }


    public Book findByTitle(String title) {
      Query query = new Query(Criteria.where("title").is(title));
      return this.mongoOps.findOne(query, Book.class,
        BOOK_COLLECTION);

    }


    public void update(Book p) {
      this.mongoOps.save(p, BOOK_COLLECTION);
    }


    public int deleteByTitle(String title) {
      Query query = new Query(Criteria.where("title").is(title));
      WriteResult result = this.mongoOps.remove(query, Book.class,
        BOOK_COLLECTION);
      return result.getN();
    }

  }
```

In Spring 2.0 and later, the @Repository annotation is a marker for any class that fulfills the role or stereotype of a repository (also known as DAO).

Within our BookDAOImpl class, we have provided some wrapper methods for adding (create) or updating (update) documents. The findByTitle method shows an example of how to use the criteria API to perform searches over your collections of data. In the next section, we will see some more complex examples using multiple conditions in our query.

Once configured, MongoOperations is thread-safe and can be re-used across multiple instances.

Adding the Application class

The `Application` class will not be much different from the one coded in the repository section. We will need to wire the DAO class in our code and execute the methods to create our collection of books:

```java
package com.packtpub.mongo.chapter6.template;

import org.springframework.beans.factory.annotation.Autowired;
import org.springframework.boot.CommandLineRunner;
import org.springframework.boot.SpringApplication;
import org.springframework.boot.autoconfigure.SpringBootApplication;

@SpringBootApplication
public class Application implements CommandLineRunner {

  @Autowired
  BookDAO bookDAO;

  public static void main(String[] args) {
    SpringApplication.run(Application.class, args);
  }

  @Override
  public void run(String... args) throws Exception {

    bookDAO.dropCollectionIfExist();
    Book b = new Book("A Tale Of Two Cities", "Charles Dickens",
      "Novel", 10);

    bookDAO.insert(b);

    Book[] books = new Book[]{
      new Book("The Da Vinci Code", "Dan Brown", "thriller", 12),
      new Book("Think and Grow Rich", "Napoleon Hill",
        "Motivational", 10),
      new Book("The Hobbit", "J.R.R. Tolkien", "Fantasy", 8),
      new Book("Le Petit Prince", "Antoine de
        Saint-Exupery","Novel", 8)
    };

    bookDAO.insertAll(books);

    Book b1 = bookDAO.findByTitle("The Hobbit");
    System.out.println("Retrieved Book=" + b1);
```

```
        b1.setPrice(6);

        bookDAO.update(b1);
        Book b2 = bookDAO.findByTitle("The Hobbit");
        System.out.println("Retrieved Book after update=" + b2);

        int count = bookDAO.deleteByTitle("Think and Grow Rich");
        System.out.println("Number of records deleted=" + count);
    }

}
```

The `Application` class uses the methods coded in `BookDAO` to perform some example CRUD operations on the database.

 Just like in the repository example, you can customize the database to be used by extending `org.springframework.data.mongodb.config.AbstractMongoConfiguration` and overriding its methods.

You can run your application using the following command:

```
mvn clean install spring-boot:run
```

As an alternative, you can right-click on the `Application` class from NetBeans and execute **Run File**.

Creating fine grained queries using Criteria

By combining the `Query` class with the `Criteria` selection, you can create complex patterns for selecting your data. This includes logical operators such as AND or NOT, for example. Here is how to select the first book, which is a `Fantasy` book and is priced less than `10`:

```
Query query = new Query();
query.addCriteria(Criteria.where("type").is("Fantasy").
  and("price").lt(10));
Book book = mongoOps.findOne(query, Book.class);
```

You can also combine multiple criteria in a single operator using `andOperator` or `orOperator`. For example, here is how to combine in a single `and` operation the type of book, and a range of price between `5` and `10`:

```
Query query = new Query();

query.addCriteria(
```

```
Criteria.where("type").is("Fantasy").andOperator(
   Criteria.where("price").gt(5),
   Criteria.where("price").lt(10)
 )
);
```

The following table shows the list of the methods that are available in the `Criteria` class (the full list of methods also includes methods to perform geospatial queries). For more information, refer to `http://docs.spring.io/spring-data/mongodb/docs/current/reference/html/#repositories.query-methods`.

Function	Description
`Criteria all (Object o)`	This is the criteria using the `$all` operator
`Criteria and (String key)`	This adds a chained criteria with the specified key to the current criteria and returns the newly created one
`Criteria andOperator (Criteria... criteria)`	This creates an and query using the `$and` operator for all of the provided criteria (this requires MongoDB 2.0 or later)
`Criteria elemMatch (Criteria c)`	This is the criteria using the `$elemMatch` operator
`Criteria exists (boolean b)`	This criteria uses the `$exists` operator
`Criteria gt (Object o)`	This criteria uses the `$gt` operator
`Criteria gte (Object o)`	This criteria uses the `$gte` operator
`Criteria in (Object... o)`	This criteria uses the `$in` operator for a `var args` argument.
`Criteria in (Collection<?> collection)`	This criteria uses the `$in` operator using a collection
`Criteria is (Object o)`	This criteria uses the `$is` operator
`Criteria lt (Object o)`	This criteria uses the `$lt` operator
`Criteria lte (Object o)`	This criteria uses the `$lte` operator
`Criteria mod (Number value, Number remainder)`	This criteria uses the `$mod` operator
`Criteria ne (Object o)`	This criteria uses the `$ne` operator
`Criteria nin (Object... o)`	This criteria uses the `$nin` operator
`Criteria norOperator (Criteria... criteria)`	This creates a nor query using the `$nor` operator for all of the provided criteria
`Criteria not ()`	This criteria uses the `$not` meta operator, which affects the following clause

Function	Description
`Criteria orOperator (Criteria… criteria)`	This creates an or query using the `$or` operator for all of the provided criteria
`Criteria regex (String re)`	This criteria uses a `$regex` operator
`Criteria size (int s)`	This criteria uses the `$size` operator
`Criteria type (int t)`	This criteria uses the `$type` operator

Finally, just like we have discussed in the *Using the Spring repository to access MongoDB* section of this chapter, you can provide a MongoDB JSON-based query to your `MongoOperations` interface. In this case, you will need to use one of its subclasses called `BasicQuery`. The following example shows how to perform the same selection introduced at the beginning of this chapter using a JSON query:

```
BasicQuery query1 = new BasicQuery("{ price : { $lt : 10 }, type :
    'Fantasy' }");
Book book = mongoOps.findOne(query1, Book.class);
```

Summary

This chapter completed our journey through the libraries, which can manage persistence on MongoDB. We have gone through the Spring Data project, which can be easily combined with the new Spring Boot framework to create a persistence layer with very little code and no configuration at all. We have covered the two main approaches that you can use, that is creating repository interfaces, which are able to derive DB statements directly from the field name of your documents, or using `MongoTemplate`, which provides a fine grained approach to your data persistence.

The two approaches are, however, not mutually exclusive, which means you can combine the best of the two approaches in your applications using common constructs, such as the Query and the Criteria APIs.

Index

Thank you for buying
MongoDB for Java Developers

About Packt Publishing

Packt, pronounced 'packed', published its first book, *Mastering phpMyAdmin for Effective MySQL Management*, in April 2004, and subsequently continued to specialize in publishing highly focused books on specific technologies and solutions.

Our books and publications share the experiences of your fellow IT professionals in adapting and customizing today's systems, applications, and frameworks. Our solution-based books give you the knowledge and power to customize the software and technologies you're using to get the job done. Packt books are more specific and less general than the IT books you have seen in the past. Our unique business model allows us to bring you more focused information, giving you more of what you need to know, and less of what you don't.

Packt is a modern yet unique publishing company that focuses on producing quality, cutting-edge books for communities of developers, administrators, and newbies alike. For more information, please visit our website at www.packtpub.com.

About Packt Open Source

In 2010, Packt launched two new brands, Packt Open Source and Packt Enterprise, in order to continue its focus on specialization. This book is part of the Packt Open Source brand, home to books published on software built around open source licenses, and offering information to anybody from advanced developers to budding web designers. The Open Source brand also runs Packt's Open Source Royalty Scheme, by which Packt gives a royalty to each open source project about whose software a book is sold.

Writing for Packt

We welcome all inquiries from people who are interested in authoring. Book proposals should be sent to author@packtpub.com. If your book idea is still at an early stage and you would like to discuss it first before writing a formal book proposal, then please contact us; one of our commissioning editors will get in touch with you.

We're not just looking for published authors; if you have strong technical skills but no writing experience, our experienced editors can help you develop a writing career, or simply get some additional reward for your expertise.

MongoDB Cookbook

ISBN: 978-1-78216-194-3   Paperback: 388 pages

Over 80 practical recipes to design, deploy, and administer MongoDB

1. Gain a thorough understanding of some of the key features of MongoDB.

2. Learn the techniques necessary to solve frequent MongoDB problems.

3. Packed full of step-by-step recipes to help you with installation, design, and deployment.

Learning MongoDB [Video]

ISBN: 978-1-78398-392-6   Duration: 03:26 hrs

A comprehensive guide to using MongoDB for ultra-fast, fault tolerant management of big data, including advanced data analysis

1. Master MapReduce and the MongoDB aggregation framework for sophisticated manipulation of large sets of data.

2. Manage databases and collections, including backup, recovery, and security.

3. Discover how to secure your data using SSL, both from the client and via programming languages.

Please check **www.PacktPub.com** for information on our titles

www.ingramcontent.com/pod-product-compliance
Lightning Source LLC
Chambersburg PA
CBHW060131060326
40690CB00018B/3830